WHY YOU DRINK AND
HOW TO STOP

A JOURNEY TO
FREEDOM

VERONICA VALLI

Addictions Therapist and Recovered Alcoholic

Consultant Editor: Annemarie Young

Published by
Ebby Publishing
www.ebbypublishing.com

Disclaimer

The information contained in this book is based on the personal and
professional experiences of the author. It is not intended as a substitute
for consulting with your physician or other healthcare professional.
The author and publisher are not responsible for any adverse side effects or consequences resulting directly or indirectly from the use of
any of the suggestions discussed in this book. All matters pertaining
to your individual health should be supervised by a healthcare professional. Some of the names and locations of the people and clients
mentioned in this book have been changed to protect their identity.

About the Author

Veronica Valli, Addictions Therapist, NLP Prac, Ad Dip, MASC
Life Coach, EFT Prac

Veronica has worked as a therapist and life coach specialising in addiction for over ten years; her experience includes working with young people in the criminal justice system, primary care adult treatment, outreach services and private practice. Veronica has also worked in local government, delivering local drug and alcohol strategies.

As a recovered alcoholic and drug addict, she has personal experience of what it takes to recover from an addiction. Veronica struggled with alcoholism through most of her twenties. As a binge drinker, she was aware for some time that something was wrong but was unable to define what it was; a chance meeting led to her finally getting help and turning her life around.

At the height of her addiction, Veronica was unable to go to work without the aid of a drink; her life and confidence were in tatters. She got sober in 2000 at the age of twenty-seven. She now uses this experience to help and inspire others. She fully believes that all alcoholics and addicts can recover if they have access to the right kind of help, and that they can then go on to live life to the full.

She is committed to educating and informing the public on problem drinking and addiction and has appeared regularly on BBC Radio Cambridgeshire as a specialist guest. She has appeared on the Lorraine Kelly show on ITV, and an ITV programme entitled *The Truth About*

Binge Drinking; she has also appeared in national magazines and publications, discussing recovery from alcoholism.

Veronica is married with a young son and is currently working in private practice.

http://veronicavalli.com
http://twitter.com/veronicavalli
https://www.facebook.com/addictionexpert

About the Consultant Editor

Annemarie Young, Writer and publishing consultant, BAHons, DipEd, MSc, MA

Annemarie has worked in publishing for almost thirty years: as a senior editor in a major university publishing house in the UK for the first twenty years, and after that as an editorial consultant for a number of large publishers.

She also writes books for young children learning to read, and is co-author of an acclaimed non-fiction series for older children. She is Editor of the alumni magazine for a University of Cambridge graduate college.

Praise for *Why You Drink and How to Stop*

Chip Somers, *CEO of Focus12 Treatment Centre* www.focus12.co.uk

For the first time, all the relevant information and help for the struggling alcoholic or addict is in one place. Too often all this valuable help and guidance is scattered about in many places. This book brings it all together and forms a perfect handbook. It also provides guidance for the 'forgotten' people in this matter – the family and friends. This book should be compulsory for every doctor's surgery. It is direct, to the point, and easy to read and access. Focus12 will be using it to back up much of its work.

Rosalind Bubb, *Dip Clin Hyp MNLP Coach, EFT, TAT Professional* www.rosalindb.com

Do you think you might have a problem with drink?
Does someone you care about have one?
Do you want to understand what's going on, and find a way out?
Then this book is for you.
Facing up to a life without alcohol can be a very frightening prospect. As a recovered alcoholic and drug addict, Veronica Valli has personal experience of what it takes to recover. In this friendly and life-changing book Veronica will guide you step by step through a practical approach to stopping.
Why You Drink and How To Stop is straightforward, grounded, and inspiring. The first section of the book looks at and deals with the three-part DISEASE of alcoholism and why it is crucial that all three parts are addressed. The second section looks at the PROBLEM: the drivers and

pathway to alcoholism. The third section is about the SOLUTION: getting the help you need and the early stages of recovery from alcoholism; it addresses the psychological and spiritual aspects of recovery.

The next two chapters are about how a sober alcoholic deals with relationships, and are also for those *in relationship with* an alcoholic – as a parent, partner or friend. The last chapter is about becoming the best possible version of yourself.

All in all, this book de-mystifies the experience of alcoholism. It maps out a clear approach to recovery, and will support you through that process. It leaves you with hope, and a clear way forward. It is both inspirational and practical. It could be just what you are looking for.

Darlene Steelman, *Recovering alcoholic and author of The Daily Woman* (www.thedailywoman.wordpress.com). Recognised as a 'Truly Exceptional Alcohol Addiction Resource' by www.kwikmed.org/

I have always been sceptical of books that tell me how I can 'stop' doing things. As a recovering alcoholic well into my sixth year of sobriety, the only books I have ever read on alcoholism are *The Big Book, Came to Believe* and a host of other AA approved literature found on the tables at meetings.

As I read 'About the Author' I was excited. When I was in early recovery, I found that the best counsellors at my group sessions were men and women who had been through the struggles of alcoholism and addiction. Counsellors who had not experienced the turmoil of being sick and tired on a daily basis and going back for more did not possess the empathy that addicts and alcoholics require.

The book is broken down into three parts, comprising ten chapters in all. The author's story comes first and hooked me from the outset.

Part 1 is all about alcoholism: the disease and the attendant madness. I got a lot out of Part 1 because I could relate to a lot of the shared thoughts and feelings. Anybody unsure about whether they are drinking alcoholically or not should take a look at the section 'The cost of drinking'. I highlighted a lot here, and throughout this book.

Part 2 addresses 'The Problem'. The problem of course is the 'why' of alcoholism. There is an emptiness in an active alcoholic, and Veronica touches on it perfectly. She writes a lot about our 'spirit' and living our truth. There is also much about emotions, fear and behaviour.

Part 3, 'The Solution', fascinated me. One of the most interesting parts of the book is the 'farewell letter to alcohol'. I enjoyed that letter and the idea of writing the letter as if ending a destructive love affair. There is a chapter on how to deal with friends who still drink, the spiritual aspect of recovery and lots of questions to think about.

Throughout the book I highlighted many parts as I wrote notes in the margin. The talk about Alcoholics Anonymous is refreshing because the programme has been around for decades and any alcoholic I know who has worked through an honest and rigorous programme is still sober and happy today.

The stories of other alcoholics' experiences, strength and hope, are inspiring too. As alcoholics, we tend to think no one has gone through what we have, or felt the way we feel or lost the things we've lost. The stories scattered through Veronica's book show this is untrue and give a message of hope and possibility.

I definitely recommend this book as an aid to *The Big Book* and the programme of Alcoholics Anonymous.

Alexander McKinlay, *Recovering alcoholic and addictions therapist at The Living Room, Stevenage, UK* www.thelivingroom.me.uk

Why You drink and How to Stop is a must-read, user-friendly, thorough, and practical book that will help alcoholics, their families and friends, as well as any therapist working with alcoholics, to understand the alcoholic personality. It also provides practical steps to recovery, steps that anyone can follow.

This book is written by an alcoholic/addict in recovery, who is also a therapist specialising in addiction. She uses personal experience and an understanding of what being an active alcoholic and an alcoholic in recovery is all about. This book includes chapters on what alcoholism is, alcoholic behaviour, binge drinking, denial, and emotional unmanageability. It also includes chapters on 'The Solution', which deal with, among other things, interventions, getting help, Alcoholics Anonymous, abstinence, overcoming blocks, understanding emotions, dealing with the past, spiritual aspects, relationship patterns and co-dependence. The author also tackles issues like the dry drunk syndrome, emotional immaturity, and relationships with an active alcoholic. It does not appear to miss anything relevant to alcoholism and its treatment.

Veronica Valli has written a comprehensive book on alcoholism, addiction and recovery. In this book, she shares what really works when it comes to getting sober and staying sober. I am glad she has. Read this book if you're an alcoholic or addict and don't know how to get sober and clean, or you know someone who is still suffering. This is an inspiring read, and I highly recommend it.

Reverend Linda Carter

The honesty and integrity of Veronica's book are testament to her work and life. The transparency of her personal experience will encourage and inspire anyone who reads it, giving them courage and confidence that she has 'been there, done that' and found her way back to her true self. She shows anyone how they can do the same.

I liked Veronica's writing style. I found her direct dialogue with the reader refreshing. I felt that she was personally speaking to me – intimately, powerfully and at the same time, providing a comfortable and accessible read.

The personal stories are heartfelt and bring a strong sense of reality. I particularly liked the love letter to alcohol and have not come across anything quite like this before.

Addiction in many forms is rife in our society and this much needed book will reach out to many and help them understand the progression, destruction and recovery from addiction.

This is a practical, useable and workable guide to recovery, which is the result of the experience and insights of a highly experienced and exceptionally skilled therapist.

I read this book in one sitting but have read it over and over again. I recommend it to anyone with a need to know more about this subject.

Dedication

This book is dedicated to:
Bill W and Bob S – for sharing the solution
John J – who showed me how
Heather M – for seeing who I really was
Rob V – who loves what I became
Xavier V – who is the greatest joy I have ever known

Acknowledgements

WOULD FIRSTLY LIKE to thank my husband, who effectively marched me to the computer and made me write this book. I would also like to thank him for his complete and utter support for everything I do.

I would like to mention Mindy Gibbons Klien, aka The Book Midwife, who helped me kick off the planning process.

The material from this book has been drawn from my experience as an alcoholic, addictions therapist and from extensive research. I would like to acknowledge Anthony Robbins' contributions to the study of human excellence, as his work demonstrates how we think and how we deal with our feelings. This has been very pertinent in my research on alcoholism. I would also like to acknowledge Pia Mellody and Melody Beattie for their research into the field of co-dependency. I have drawn on many masters of personal development, therapy, life coaching and recovery, whose knowledge and wisdom have entered the general consciousness; I have credited these people wherever possible.

Annemarie Young deserves a medal for bombarding potential publishers with emails and phone calls; simply, without her efforts this book would never have seen the light of day and for that I am eternally grateful. Her gifts as an editor have made this book better than I could ever have done alone. I've enjoyed working with her more than I can put into words and am honoured that she has also become my friend. I also want to thank Tony Robinson for his read throughs, insights and suggestions, which also raised this book up to another level. Not only is he a fabulous writer, he is an extraordinary cook and wonderful friend.

Without John and Sue Jones this book would never have happened; their unconditional love and support literally saved my life. Their wisdom, love and insight are scattered throughout this book.

Liz Jasper gave me wonderful insights and shone a light on all the areas that needed polishing. Many thanks for her continued support and time, both are enormously appreciated. I'd like to thank Kendra Leighton for her read through and Orya Blumenfeld for his continued IT support, without which I would surely be certifiable by now.

Sarah Gillespie, Emma Gawlinski and Linzi Hudson were my angels who loved me no matter what, who always saw something better inside me. It is ordinary acts of love and kindness from friends who should have abandoned us that sometimes makes the difference as to whether an alcoholic lives or dies. You three girls made that difference for me.

I am also beyond blessed to have amazing people who have come across my path in their search for recovery; you have enriched me more than you can possibly imagine and are my brothers and sisters in this wonderful journey we are on.

Lastly, I would like to thank the wonderful people who gave me permission to use their case studies in this book. Your courage and tenacity have left me speechless. It's an honour to walk this path with you. Thank you for letting me include your stories as testimony that what we have is not unique to us, that recovery is possible to all who search.

Contents

Foreword by Danielle Lloyd

FROM THE OUTSIDE I know my life may have looked 'perfect' to some people. I was a beauty queen and model, photographed at glamorous parties, dating a footballer. People envied me. I should have been happy, but instead I was miserable.

My life seemed to be spinning out of control; I felt lonely and rejected and was using alcohol and drugs to cope.

I had hit 'rock bottom'.

Thank God I did, because it was when I was in my darkest place that I finally got some help. I started seeing Veronica in 2008 and immediately felt that she was someone who could help me. She listened to me and helped me make sense of my past and the choices I had made. I still had dark days and never thought I would get through, but Veronica continued to believe in me and I finally began to believe I could. Because of abusive relationships I've had in the past it's been hard for me to trust people, but I trusted Veronica. In many ways Veronica knows me better than I know myself; she has seen me at my worst and taught me how to overcome my challenges. I feel so much stronger and more confident through the work we have done together. I made the decision to stop self-destructing and turned my life around. I am still a model and go to glamorous parties, but I am also a wife and mother now and that is the role that is most important to me. I really believe I have the life I have now because of Veronica's help.

I would urge anyone who is struggling, especially with alcohol or drug problems, to read this book. It could change your life, like it did mine.

Best wishes,
Danielle Lloyd
Model, TV personality, wife and mother

Introduction

My story

I AM A RECOVERED alcoholic. I have been sober since 26 May, 2000. I have personally experienced the pain and degradation that alcoholism can cause, as well as the joys of recovery. As a qualified addictions therapist in the UK, I have worked with hundreds of clients seeking a way out of the hell that they are living – unable to understand why they can't control their drinking or how things ever got this bad. And, more to the point, what they were going to do about it.

I drank alcohol for years and got sober at the age of twenty-seven, when I finally realised I was dying on the inside as well as the outside. I knew I had to drastically change my life.

But how had it come to this?

On the outside my life looked 'normal'. I had been to University. I always had good jobs. I'd never been arrested, fired or expelled from anywhere. I had lots of friends and was well travelled. On the outside everything looked OK. On the inside I was falling apart.

No matter what I did or where I went or who I was with, I had a desperate feeling deep inside me that never went away. Namely, that I didn't fit in, was 'less than' everybody else, and I had an overriding fear that I simply didn't know how to 'do life'.

Alcohol was the only thing that ever gave me comfort. But of course, it created a whole new set of problems: I did and said things when I was drunk that I felt deeply ashamed about. I became someone I didn't like or respect. I hated myself. So I just drank and drank because the alcohol worked like an anaesthetic. It helped me fit in, not feel 'less than'. It numbed the pain of my thoughts and feelings, for a while at least.

My personal experience

I tried to drink like 'other people' because they looked 'normal' to me. Other people drank and they were fine; I could tell. I would judge them by how they looked on the outside and I wanted to be like that.

Something inside me was different and it wasn't fine. Which is why I had to lie to myself – a big fat lie that ate me up and that I had to keep telling myself, because it kept a lid on the horror. I had to lie about what I was doing to myself. I had to lie about how I really felt. I had to lie about who I was. I had to lie because I was terrified of the horror inside me being exposed.

This may only make sense to someone who has had a problem with drink or any other mood or mind-altering substance. Or it may make sense to you if you have lived a life of desperate compromise and unfulfilled promise.

Do you understand?

Have you got secrets inside you?

Do you have to lie too?

Do you know what it's like to live with such a denial of your truth that you wake up every morning in despair and feel like your soul is lying on the floor next to you and you have no idea how you are supposed to make it through the day, let alone through life?

I just couldn't figure out how everyone else lived. How were they doing life? How come it was so easy for them?

I know I was born this way. I never felt right. I always felt that I was looking at you through a glass screen. I was on one side, alone, and everyone else was on the other side.

I've always felt wrong. I would measure myself up against people. I would always come up lacking, so I'd just try harder to be like them. I wanted my insides to feel like their outsides looked. So I drank and drank. I didn't know there was another way to live this life.

And for a while, the burning pain inside me stopped because alcohol numbed everything. However, it took me further and further away from my truth; from who I was and could be.

Alcohol wasn't killing me. Alcohol was holding me together.

But alcohol was only a symptom of the problem. The *problem* was within me. And, as I was to learn, so was the *solution*.

Let's begin.

PART 1

ALCOHOLISM

Alcoholism is a physical, psychological and spiritual disease. All three of these components have to be understood if they are to be addressed in the alcoholic.

Alcoholism is not (necessarily) binge drinking or even heavy drinking, but these can lead to a dangerous breakdown of inhibitions, with the attendant consequences, and in some cases, to alcoholism.

Chapter 1

What is alcoholism?

Alcoholism a disease in three parts

ALCOHOLISM IS A condition that has baffled society for hundreds of years. Up until the 1950s, alcoholism was perceived as a moral disorder or a failure of will power. Alcoholics were seen as immoral, weak-willed or degenerate and were treated with scorn and contempt.

This began to change with the emergence of Alcoholics Anonymous, and medical research into the causes and conditions of alcoholism. It was E M Jellinek's work in the 1950s that introduced the concept of alcoholism as a disease with particular symptoms. In *Concepts of Chemical Dependency* (2012), Harold Doweiko explores whether there is a genetic predisposition towards alcoholism and addiction, or if there are biological differences between individuals who become addicted and those that don't. The truth is that we don't yet know to what extent alcoholism and addiction are due to 'nature' or to 'nurture'. It seems that both biology and circumstances can contribute to whether someone becomes an alcoholic.

There is an important argument about personal choice and responsibility, and it is also said that no one puts a gun to an alcoholic's head and forces them to drink. At some point we choose to drink, we are not forced to.

There is merit in all these points, but this is not what this book is about. I am certainly a believer in personal responsibility, but I believe that biology and circumstance both contribute to the development of alcoholism. I don't believe we can ascribe 'fault', as the conditions for developing alcoholism are mostly set up in childhood. These are issues I will explore later. I do believe that instead of getting lost in the 'why' you are an alcoholic, it's far more important to figure out what you are going to do about it. Because once an individual has crossed the line into destructive drinking or drug use, it *is* their responsibility to do something about it.

And for alcoholics, the *problem* and the *solution* both lie within.

I believe, as do many others, that alcoholism is a three-part disease or illness, comprising:

- physical addiction
- psychological craving and obsession
- spiritual illness.

As with any disease, it can be fatal to treat one part of the disease and ignore the rest. This is particularly true of alcoholism. In treating alcoholism, all three aspects of the illness must be treated in order to have a successful outcome. However, the most important part, and the part that is often ignored, is the 'spiritual illness'. There can be some resistance to accepting that alcoholism is primarily a 'disease of the spirit,' but it is actually the most critical factor and can explain the insidiousness, denial and insanity of the illness far more effectively than the other factors.

To the casual observer, alcoholism seems like pure insanity; it's incomprehensible, as the drinker self-destructs again and again, yet still refuses to see the part of alcohol in this, or indeed to see alcohol as the cause. This is because it is very difficult for an alcoholic to just stop drinking without outside help – just as it is difficult to treat any other disease without help.

Not every alcoholic is necessarily physically dependent. Physical dependence on alcohol is apparent when a drinker displays withdrawal symptoms and increased tolerance to alcohol. Doweiko discusses how the alcoholic has to drink in order to *feel* normal. As well as the physical dependence, the physically dependent user will also be tolerant to alcohol. This means they will need to drink more and more to get the same effects. The body physically adapts to having alcohol always inside it. When the alcohol is withdrawn, the body must adapt again. When this stage is reached, a medical intervention is required to safely detox from alcohol.

Psychological dependence occurs when the user habitually uses alcohol to cope with their emotions and feelings. The user may not yet be physically addicted to alcohol, but is clearly pre-occupied and obsessed with alcohol as the 'solution' to their circumstances and feelings. The user comes to believe that they *need* alcohol. It is the primary thing in their life, the solution to all their problems and the accompaniment to all situations. They will convince themselves they can handle one or two drinks, but end up having far more, despite their intentions or promises. It's almost as if they are drinking *against their will*. The alcohol is in charge. In spite of themselves, the opportunity to drink is never passed up despite the consequences of this beginning to add up. Without realising it, the alcoholic has lost control of when and how much they drink.

Then there is the spiritual illness, which I would argue is the most important and the least understood. For many people, there is a confusion over the meaning of spirituality. Spirituality is not the same as religion. Religions can and do contain elements of spirituality, but religion is not necessarily spiritual.

The terms 'spirit' or 'spiritual' refer to the voice inside us – the voice that makes us unique and is the basis for who we are and who we become. It is the part of ourselves that loves, hopes, dreams and hurts. Our feelings stem from our spirit and its unique response to the world. It is the part of us as human beings you can't put under a microscope, but we all know is there. And it is the part of ourselves that most of us know least about, let alone know how to manage. It is our *internal experience*. With alcoholics, this 'spirit' is wounded and in pain.

How this comes about is complex and will be explored in later chapters. But like a physical pain, it won't be ignored and will beg for our attention until we treat it. For alcoholics it is this deep emotional pain that is so hard to describe or articulate. It just feels that something deep down is 'wrong'. When someone persistently feels this way, they naturally look for a 'cure' or a fix. Alcoholics choose alcohol.

Alcoholism is an 'internal condition'

My work with alcoholics and my own experience has shown me that alcoholism is an internal condition, one that takes root in our thoughts and feelings before eventually becoming expressed in our behaviour. This book will explore the internal, or spiritual, experience of the alcoholic and show why this is essential in understanding alcoholism. It is only with this knowledge that *recovery* becomes possible.

The themes explored here are not unique to alcoholics. I believe they are universal in their scope. I also believe, based on our behaviour, that the world in general is suffering from a form of spiritual illness, and that alcoholism is merely one example of this.

Our culture has become focused on the external factors of our existence. We over-emphasise the importance of what we look like, where we work, what we have and what others think about us – to the detriment of our internal experience, and to such an extent that not many of us know how to manage our internal experience, or understand its significance and its impact on our external experience.

If you understand, as many in the field do, that our behaviour is a manifestation of our inner experience, then we can see that the destructive things we do are a reflection of inner turmoil and pain.

Alcoholism is an extreme version of this, but only one version. The effects of an unsatisfactory internal experience are apparent in many ways: over-consumption, obsessive focus on appearance, all forms of addiction, overspending/debt, eating disorders, obesity, etc.

Are these not just behavioural patterns we have developed to cope with how we feel about, and deal with, our feelings and the world at large?

Throughout history human beings have had the urge to fix or change the way they feel, to escape or enhance reality. And for some, no price is too high to pay for the experience.

There is something so attractive and seductive about the effects of alcohol that we are able to ignore, rationalise or even glamorise the destruction it has caused throughout history. We look back on our history with alcohol, both personally and collectively, with rose-tinted romanticism, refusing to see the deadly grip it maintains over those who surrender to its creeping ability to distort our truth.

Such is the power of alcohol that we have become able, to an astonishing degree, to tell ourselves massive lies, in order to keep doing what we are doing. Even when it's gone way beyond the point of having fun, even when we know it's destroying us. We alcoholics are able to lie to ourselves in such a way that we can continue to self-destruct, lead miserable and unfulfilled lives, and all the time telling ourselves we don't have a problem.

It isn't alcohol that kills alcoholics. It's the lies they tell themselves in order to keep doing what they are doing. If they didn't lie to themselves, the pain of the reality would be unbearable. Why is it we would rather drink to the point of destruction than tell someone else how we *really* feel? What are we so scared of?

My story

I spent twelve years drinking and self-destructing. I still had a job and a place to live, but I felt like my insides were going black and I had no way of changing that. I kept drinking because it took away the pain. I couldn't even begin to describe my internal experience to anyone else; it hardly made sense to me. In reality, the drink worked for me for two years, then it stopped working and I began to feel even worse than I had before I started drinking.

I slowly began to die on the inside.

Anyone who has ever had a drink or drug problem or has suffered from depression will understand what that feels like. And it wasn't just the drink, drugs and nameless men I slept with that were killing me, it was the lies I had to tell myself.

I seemed to have this default programme that was set on misery and denial.

For alcoholics, there is a disjunction between *who you really are* and what you have become. Alcohol will make you into someone you do not recognise. Drinking is just one way to take away the pain of an inauthentic existence.

This book is less about drinking and more about the engine that drives drinking behaviour. It's about what's *underneath* an alcohol problem. It explores the thinking and the feelings that drive someone to abuse a harmful substance in such a way that it becomes the central most important thing in their life. It examines the fact that destructive behaviour can only be permanently changed when an emotional rearrangement takes place first. The book then, more importantly, explores the *solution*.

KINDS OF DRINKING BEHAVIOUR
Heavy drinking and binge drinking

Binge drinking is not necessarily alcoholism, although binge drinking can, over time, develop into alcoholism.

The difference between alcoholics on the one hand, and binge drinkers and heavy drinkers on the other, is that the latter can stop or moderate their drinking when their circumstances change. Most of my friends drank exactly the same way I did when we were teenagers and in their early twenties; however, when they got responsible jobs, bought houses and settled down, their drinking regulated itself: they no longer drank the way they had. An alcoholic will try, and usually succeed, in convincing themselves they are just 'heavy drinkers'. They may even be able to regulate or stop drinking for a period of time. However, they will inevitably return to the same drinking patterns as before. They can't maintain the control.

That is the difference. An alcoholic can sometimes stop drinking, *it's staying stopped that's the problem.*

Binge drinking is rarely out of the news today and in many quarters has become a desired and accepted method of drinking alcohol. There is no messing about with the intention here, binge drinkers drink to get drunk. Although binge drinking is often seen as a problem of the young, this is not necessarily the case. Binge drinking has become a 'social norm' and is prevalent across all age groups.

When I was a teenager the *whole point* of being grown up was to go out and get drunk like all the other grown ups; when you're young that's how you want to be. *Young people are copying the way they see adults drink.*

The UK Alcohol Concern Fact Sheet on young people and alcohol, 2011, quotes quotes a recent study into underage risky drinking, which found that one of the three main reasons or motivations the young people interviewed cited for their drinking were social norms and influences:

"drinking and drinking to excess was seen as part of wider social norms and the accepted culture of heavy drinking, peer influence (including peer pressure) and for greater 'respect and image' among the social group".

Because I looked old enough, I got into bars and nightclubs from the age of thirteen, as did a lot of my female peers. Make up and high heels can make a thirteen year-old look eighteen. (The legal drinking age in the UK is eighteen.) Going out and getting drunk was a very 'normal' thing to do. Our society constructed itself around the use of alcohol; it's just what you did. I ended up copying the 'grown ups' who were falling out of pubs at the weekend. I thought that's what being 'grown up' meant. It looked like fun.

And now, twelve years on, I have noticed in my work with young people how normalised excessive drinking has become for them. Overwhelmingly, young people seem to believe that the *point* of alcohol is to drink as much as it takes to get completely intoxicated. They want to binge drink, they want to get blind drunk, there is no in-between and they seem to have no regard for the dangers.

The Policeman's story

I have been a police officer for ten years and have first hand knowledge of the scale of the problems alcohol is causing. Binge drinking does not only affect the person who is drinking: it affects the taxpayer, the police, the ambulance service, and healthcare services; taxi drivers ensuring people get home safely; friends who have to drag their friends out of the gutter after being sick; parents and families who have to deal with the person through the night; cleaners who have to deal with cleaning up the vomit stained streets and picking up take-away food wrappers; and shop keepers who have to get new panes of glass because somebody decided it would be fun to smash them, just because they had had too much to drink.

Alcohol is the cause of many fights around town centres, as people are unable to control their anger, and the alcohol fuels this. It is not just testosterone-fuelled men who become monsters, but also screaming women.

More often than not, the monsters who came in for fighting or public order offences the night before are likeable people with responsibilities when they have sobered up, but alcohol simply got the better of them.

Over the years I have seen so many incidents involving people drinking, from the alcoholics who can't control their bodily functions, to people fighting and causing serious harm to one another just because they were unable to control themselves, to people having sex in alleyways. All because of excess drink.

It is our job to ensure these people are kept safe, but it tests your patience as a police officer and puts you off wanting to have a sensible drink yourself.

UK Police Sergeant, 36

Binge drinking and sex

I want to tell you the story of my friend Clare, who *isn't* an alcoholic but came to a realisation that her alcohol abuse led her to behave in ways she didn't understand. She is attractive, bright, successful and single. She thought her relationship with alcohol was 'normal', like that of her peers. However, her tendency to binge drink led her to behaving in ways that shattered her confidence and self esteem. This is her story.

Confessions of a binge drinker

My name is Clare, and I was a binge drinker. I wouldn't call myself an alcoholic; I've never craved a drink, never felt a compelling urge to drink on my own. But I have used alcohol to fuel my social life and take away shyness, and it has, at times, led me into trouble. As I've got older, my tolerance to alcohol has changed. When I was younger alcohol made me slightly uninhibited, but increasingly it has had the effect of completely destroying my judgement. Like the evening six months ago that is going to prey on my mind for a long time to come.

I started the evening at a party. I had a few glasses of wine, I guess. I can't really remember. I remember someone filling up my glass with champagne, then someone else giving me a cocktail. It's after that that things become hazy. My memories are a series of interconnected chunks, a jigsaw that doesn't quite fit together. What I do remember is coming out of an upstairs bathroom, where a 'friend' was waiting for me. He put his arms round me and kissed me. I kissed him back. And then I stopped, and asked him what he was doing. He was married, and was coming up to his first wedding anniversary. He and I had dated briefly a few years previously, shortly before he met his wife. But nothing came of it, and we'd never slept together. I'd all but forgotten about it.

It seemed he hadn't though. He suggested I went home with him. I reminded him he was married. He said that he and I had 'unfinished business', that we had never finished what we started all those years ago, so it wouldn't count. As the party was breaking up – and this must have been at about 4am – I realised I needed to get home. My 'friend' came to find me and said I could take a taxi from his place. It seemed reasonable enough as an idea so I went back with him to his house. Quite what happened next I don't know. My next memory is lying on his sofa, kissing him, then his undoing my bra. And by that time, I didn't care. I'd forgotten my earlier objections and was only aware of being kissed by an attractive man. But I did raise my objections again, when he suggested we had sex. I remember saying no, saying again, 'but you're married'. And I can't remember what he said, but it was something persuasive. He carried on kissing me. He took off the rest of my clothes. And somewhere, around about 6am, he fucked me over one of his sofas.

Does that sound coarse? But I can't call it anything else. There was no emotion. And I can't call it sex, either, because it was hardly an interactive experience; a few seconds of him satisfying his ego. I don't think I can call this rape because at some point I had agreed to it, at some point, when he had argued away my protestations about his being married, I stopped protesting; but I was thinking with my body not my brain.

(Author's note: What happened to Clare is rape and is recognised as such in law. The victim offered countless protestations, but was not in charge of her faculties and was worn down by the perpetrator – her intoxication had rendered her incapable of making a choice. The reason that Clare herself says she doesn't think she can call this rape is because, as you will see, she believes she should take responsibility for the intoxication which made her incapable of following through on her original decision to say 'no' firmly.)

It took me weeks to stop feeling dirty. For my part, I believe I have to take responsibility for what I did. For whatever state I was in at six that morning, I knew what I was doing when I kissed him, when I kissed my friend's husband, when I let myself kiss him and enjoy it and convinced myself it was OK. It was me who got so drunk, me who failed to follow the limits I'd set, me who over-indulged in a drug that I know can change one's state of mind and corrupt a person's powers to decide, and therefore, that pointless, degrading moment of drunken intercourse is something for which I can only, in all fairness, blame myself.

Clare, 38

Clare had a huge wakeup call and because of this she stopped drinking altogether for a while and examined her behaviour. She was shocked and frightened as the behaviour went completely against her values and beliefs; she was not this kind of person and yet she had acted this way. It confused her and her self-esteem took a huge battering.

What bothers me the most about Clare's story is that it is far from unusual. In fact, I would hazard a guess that this is almost a regular occurrence throughout Britain and the USA most weekends, ordinary people who have fallen into binge drinking and casual sex because that's just what everyone else is doing.

By normalising our drinking behaviour we feel as if we have minimised the dangers and risks and justified our consumption by representing it as something else.

Who, me?

One of the ways that this is done, by the individual, is to justify our consumption compared to *other* people. From the perspective of a binge drinker, when *everyone* is drinking this way, it surely *must* be OK? It seems that because so many people are drinking to excess, we have collectively decided that this is normal, acceptable behaviour. This is a common way to rationalise away the risk. We all then collude in this deception.

I hear these statements all the time in my practice:

- Everybody's doing it, so why can't I?
- I'm not as bad as them.
- I don't drink during the week.
- It's only a problem if you have to have a drink.
- But everyone drinks.

Binge drinking has become normal drinking and it is destroying what's good about alcohol: the right kind of wine with food, for instance or, occasionally, to unwind after a stressful day. One whisky is normal, not five.

Alcohol can be an aid to having fun, *but is not fun of itself.* It's the result, not the objective. For the alcoholic, it becomes the objective. This is what I take most issue with, that at some point in our culture we have created a belief system that alcohol is *how* we have fun. And that it is the *only* way to have fun.

The number one lament I hear in my practice is: *But how will I have fun without alcohol?* You will, trust me. You will have more fun than you ever had before.

Alcoholism and binge drinking are two separate, but very related problems. It is the dishonesty around binge drinking that alarms me the most. The horrible consequences of this behaviour that we have normalised are something we are only just beginning to talk about.

The cost of drinking

I started as a binge drinker and my drinking quickly progressed to psychological dependence. My drinking was fun only between the ages of fifteen and seventeen.

While it lasted I had a great time; I loved alcohol and I had a great time drinking. I lived for the weekends. I loved the excitement and build up before a night out. I loved the feeling of adventure that anything could happen, that anything was possible. The night felt magical. I loved getting dressed up with my girlfriends. I loved meeting friends in the pub and that first tingle of excitement of the first drink. A hangover seemed to be a small price to pay for how good it all felt.

For those two years I was a binge drinker and recreational drug user. It was brilliant.

I really had fun. I know I did. *But*, this is what it cost me:

- I left home at sixteen because being there impinged on my drinking and drug use.
- I lived off state benefits.
- I barely passed my exams.
- I stayed in an emotionally, physically and mentally abusive relationship with another binge drinker and drug user.
- I cut myself off from all of my school friends and family and therefore had zero emotional support.
- I was sick every time I was hung-over, which was often.
- I was often late for work.
- I had no money, no savings.
- I couldn't afford driving lessons like all of my friends.
- I couldn't afford anything – all my money went on drink.
- I lost a baby-sitting job and the friendship of the family because I got so drunk in their brother-in-law's pub he had to throw a bucket of water over me, as I lay in the gutter outside his pub covered in vomit. They said they couldn't trust me with their children after that.
- I had intense, uncomfortable, insincere friendships that could never translate into real friendships when we were sober.
- I had fair weather friends.

- I was friends with people I didn't like very much.
- I often felt lonely even though I was surrounded by people.
- I often felt left out even though I was in the middle of everything.
- I lost my dignity. People laughed at me, not with me.
- I vastly under-achieved in my studies and work.
- I didn't come close to fulfilling my potential.
- Nobody told me I had any potential.
- I tried drugs without any thought of the effects or consequences.
- I had sex with men I didn't like because I thought I would be loved.
- I moved house five times in two years.
- I secretly wanted to get pregnant so I would be 'safe' and could get a flat and some money and would not have to cope with doing anything with my life.
- I had an affair with my boyfriend's best friend and broke up their friendship and the band they were in.
- The goalposts of my integrity were moved on a weekly basis as I began to behave in a way I didn't understand.
- I learnt that living was about coping and not showing anyone how I really felt.

I became false, fake, shallow, empty and lost, with no words to tell anyone how I felt.

I was never physically dependent on alcohol. I didn't require a medical detox when I finally stopped. I was, however, extremely psychologically dependent on alcohol and was very, very spiritually ill. Alcohol was central to my existence and my life revolved around it. It always seemed like the answer for me.

Initially, the feelings alcohol gave me seemed to far outweigh the price I had to pay. Until finally, the price was too high. I vaguely realised I was drinking too much and that my behaviour was out of control, but I kept finding ways to justify it to myself. Then one day I just couldn't any more, I couldn't hide from myself any longer. I had to get help.

I realised there were two paths in life. One was to live your truth and one was not to. I saw that I had not been living mine, and the pain of that almost killed me, because at the end, even drink couldn't take the pain away. I was either going to die or make the choice to live authentically without alcohol, no matter how hard that seemed at the time. It was this realisation that enabled me to get help and to get sober. It wasn't easy at first, although ironically it was so much easier than the life I had been living up to then. Before I knew it, my life changed and I never looked back. I never missed drinking or what it gave me.

Recovery starts when we come to the realisation that we can't continue the way we have been, and *we ask for help.*

PART 2

THE PROBLEM

Chapter 2

The path to alcoholism

Alcoholism can be described as a spiritual disjunction, which alcoholics try to fix by rearranging their outside circumstances. They are able to maintain their delusion through many forms of lying and denial. The end result of this behaviour is that alcoholics forget who they really are.

THIS CHAPTER WILL discuss how it is the suffering of the 'spirit' that is ultimately at the core of alcoholism and addiction.

"Since ancient times philosophers have suggested that there exists within each of us a spark of divine light, which was called spiritus by the ancient Romans. Once it is extinguished the light of that individual's life is lost forever." Doweiko, 2012

It is my intention to explore in detail the concept of spirituality as a key to understanding alcoholism. The 'internal condition' or 'internal experience,' is what is deep inside us; it is vital for all of us to understand ourselves from the inside out. Understanding our internal experience is how we understand what motivates our outside behaviour. I use the terms 'spiritual' and 'internal' interchangeably – to me they mean the same thing: the spiritual and internal life inside oneself. Our internal world is the voice that's inside us, the voice we wake up with and go to sleep with, the voice that gets louder when we're doing something we shouldn't be doing, the voice that sings inside when we do something which resonates with *who we really are.*

This voice is our truth. Inside us, underneath the masks, buried deep, is the real version of ourselves. Inside us is where our dreams are, our secrets, our shame, our fear, our desires, our hope, our beliefs. *They are intrinsic to our make-up. They govern everything.*

Sometimes *who we really are* scares us and we bury our true selves. We put layers over that voice so that we *don't* have to hear what it says. We ignore it because what it's saying sounds too hard for us to achieve.

"You see, the main reason so many millions of people in our world today have this spiritual malaise that they carry around with them every waking moment is because of The Integrity Gap. They're betraying themselves and not letting their true essence shine in the world. And the deepest and best parts of them certainly know it." Sharma, 2002

Spiritual malaise is that deep, deep feeling inside yourself that something is wrong; no matter what you do or where you go it doesn't seem to shift.

Internal and external factors in alcoholism

In order to overcome alcoholism, stopping the drinking of alcohol simply isn't enough. Alcoholism develops because it has an internal environment to grow in. Although external conditions enable drinking, it is the internal conditions that allow alcoholism to control someone's life. There is a need for a greater understanding of this.

- Alcoholism is an internal (spiritual) illness. Drinking is only a symptom.
- Alcoholism's key motivator is about changing how you feel.
- Alcoholism grows out of a faulty system of thinking and emotional responses.

Medically, alcoholism is often diagnosed when physical dependence is established, which means the drinker goes into physical withdrawal (which is extremely dangerous and can be life threatening) when they don't have a drink. However, it is my experience, personally and professionally, that alcoholism is a condition that exists long before dependency, or even before the first drink is even taken.

Let's look at this. Self-defeating behaviours, including alcoholism, addiction and eating disorders, have their roots in a deficient and faulty system of thinking and emotional responses, and these *existed long before any substance abuse or self-defeating behaviours started.*

This faulty system of thinking, feeling and responding establishes itself at an extremely young age. It is not the case for everyone, but commonly, you can trace an alcoholic's journey from a young age, when they began to notice and act upon a feeling of internal (spiritual) discomfort and dissatisfaction. Nearly every alcoholic I have ever worked with has described feeling 'different' when they were children.

"But for some, the accumulated insults over a lifetime become a disease in their inner world, and some turn to chemicals to fill the perceived void within or to ease their pain." Doweiko, 2012

A faulty system of thinking, and the feelings and responses that go with it, doesn't go away of its own accord. Instead, the sufferer develops coping behaviours that enable them to cope with their internal experience. The crucial factor to understand here is that the sufferer's internal experience of life is at times deeply unpleasant and uncomfortable. These feelings will then manifest as behaviours, which are visible manifestations of the unpleasant feelings. Therefore it is easy to see when surveying an alcoholic's behaviour just how dark their internal world is. Their emotions and feelings are being expressed in the destructive way they behave.

Now, these feelings can be experienced by many people who don't go on to develop alcohol problems, but it seems to be a common factor that potential alcoholics or addicts never had, or have been unable to develop, the necessary coping tools required to deal with life. Other people learn to cope, potential alcoholics don't. Potential alcoholics are born without the 'instruction manual' for living. All else follows.

Emotional maturity

I'm aware that many people feel they lack an 'instruction manual' for life, and would love a set of instructions that would ensure we always made the right decisions and took the right actions. However, with a potential alcoholic or addict, they not only lack an ability to make the best choices or decisions for themselves, they are additionally unable to learn from their mistakes, or to grow emotionally. They remain emotionally immature, which causes them even further internal distress, and they become even more self-destructive. They feel 'wrong' inside and empty; there is a near constant feeling of dissatisfaction, unhappiness, discontent or even despair, which inevitably drives them to seek ways and means to numb the pain.

Enter drugs and alcohol. These substances alter how a person feels, very quickly and very effectively. So to understand the alcoholic or addict, it is vital to understand the emotional precondition. Emotional pain is the pain we are least equipped to understand or treat. If we can't treat it then we have to kill or numb it. This is the basis for alcoholism.

From homeless alcoholic to investment banker

Matthew runs an investment bank. He's the father of a young son, and a well-liked and popular person; he is smartly dressed, good looking, articulate and intelligent. He was also a hopeless alcoholic who finally managed to get sober and deal with his internal condition.

Matthew's story

A vivid memory of alcohol and my childhood is when, whilst my family were out, I selected a pint glass, climbed into the loft of our garage and took a little bit out of each of the bottles of wine that were open, and filled the pint glass to the top. I then drank the entire pint and climbed down. I took the glass to the kitchen and went to put it in the dishwasher until I remembered that if you leave a glass that has had red wine in it upside down the wine dries, leaving a red ring on the bottom of the glass. So, I washed the glass up and put it away. I then went upstairs, brushed my teeth, sprayed deodorant on myself and sat in my room. When I realised that I had got away with it, I went and did it all again and promptly blacked out.

So these were my first drinks. My last drinks were 10% proof lagers and cheap cider at 7:30 in the morning, whilst sitting on park benches in the towns were I lived as a homeless alcoholic and drug addict. There is a clear line between these two points and it only goes down.

In the intervening period between these two points, my life is littered with failed relationships, lost families and friends, hospital stays, black outs, crime, violence, waking up in police cells covered in blood, drink driving, broken bones, near deaths, suicide attempts, homeless shelters, counselling sessions, rehabs, alcohol poisoning, borderline hypothermia, drug overdoses and so on.

The last two years of my drinking were the worst, and spent wholly on the streets. I was an aggressive, violent, egotistical, opinionated judgmental, arrogant, cocky individual. I was this way for no reason other than to keep people away from me so that (i) I could keep drinking and (ii) I would not be found out – so that no one could see that I was in fact full of fear and scared to death of everything and everyone. I had no idea how to do life.

On 4 November, 2004, I reached a physical, mental and spiritual cross roads. I was so scared of dying that I knew I had to stop drinking, but at the same time I was so scared of living life without alcohol that I could not stop drinking. This was a place of abject torture from which I could see no escape. At twenty-seven years old I was on my hands and knees in a park crying in anguish and dribbling like a feral child. I could not go on like this any more. A lady from the homeless shelter came over to me to see if she could help and all I kept saying over and over through the tears was "I want my mum, I want my mum".

I attended meetings of AA with the same gusto as I drank: more, more, more. I loved it; I loved the people, the stories and the feeling of not being alone. Life was getting better. However, the first year and a half of my recovery was some of the most painful time of my life. The reason was quite simply that putting down the drink just wasn't enough. Although I was no longer drinking, I was still an aggressive, violent, egotistical, opinionated, judgmental, arrogant, cocky individual and my life was still controlled by fear.

I reached a point after eighteen months where I realised that something had to change. I just did not want to feel like this or think like this any more. What I noticed was that there were people in some of the meetings who were completely OK with themselves and were unaffected by the good or bad opinions of others. I identified one of these individuals and asked him to show me what he had done. He took me through a programme using the specific directions outlined in *The Big Book* of Alcoholics Anonymous.

As a result of this my life has changed beyond all recognition. Fear no longer rules my life. I am completely at peace and at ease with who I am. I truly understand what it is to have a life beyond my wildest dreams.

Matthew, 34, sober since 2004

Matthew's story shows us how he used alcohol to block out his feelings and help him cope with life. It was his medication, but it failed him and it very nearly killed him. It also illustrates *that stopping drinking wasn't enough* and he had to find a way to deal with his feelings in order to *stay* sober. The results then speak for themselves. A homeless guy who turned his life around; he now runs his own company and is happily married. He will be the first to tell you that the success in his external world is as a direct result of managing his internal one.

'Hole in the Soul'

Alcoholism has also been described as a 'hole in the soul.' An emptiness deep inside as if something is missing. A feeling of never being good enough, of never feeling worthy. The majority of alcoholics I have worked with have resonated with this description. When I have a new client and I explain this concept to them, their eyes light up in recognition, it is usually the first time anyone has ever articulated to them how they feel. I believe that this 'hole in the soul' feeling can also lead to drug addiction, chronic depression, obsessive-compulsive disorder, anorexia and all manner of mental health conditions. Alcoholism is just one way it can be manifested, and rest assured, it will manifest itself. A 'hole in the soul,' or 'soul sickness', is as painful as any physical pain.

Most of the alcoholics or addicts I have worked with in my role as a therapist can relate to the 'hole in the soul' metaphor. They usually refer to this feeling or condition existing long before they tried alcohol. For me it summed up a feeling I had inside from a small child.

My story

One of the earliest memories I have is of being maybe five or six and lying perfectly still on the bathroom floor, hoping the 'wrongness' in my head would go away. I thought that if I lay perfectly still then everything would just stop. If I didn't move, I couldn't feel, and if I didn't feel it couldn't hurt. I wanted to stop 'being'; I didn't want to exist in the way that I was.

It was a very existential moment for a six year-old. I was totally, totally aware of my aloneness and my difference and it was more than I could bear in my tiny heart; I wasn't strong enough to carry that load and I had no one to turn to for help with it. Most adults don't admit to the emptiness that prevails in their own hearts, how could anyone cope with a child who was lost in hers? I saw it in my mother's eyes once, when she caught me lying on the bathroom floor, just staring. I saw that flicker of recognition deep in her eyes that immediately got buried under the sheer fear of acknowledging it.

The absolute unbearableness of being.

I know she saw it but was powerless to articulate it. What words can illustrate that dark ache that vibrates deep inside someone? I saw also the fright that a mother would feel when she saw her child behaving in that odd way, a terror of seeing a child's insides so nakedly exposed, and the darkness within them.

There isn't really a particular moment when you realise you're different from other people around you, it's more of a series of realisations that happen slowly over a period of time, accompanied by a slow creeping feeling of fear that the last thing you can ever do is reveal what is inside you to anyone else.

I was so uncomfortable in my own skin that it frightened me to think that someone else might see this. I have no idea why I felt like this; it was as though I was born with this irrational fear of anyone else seeing who I really was. I was petrified of it.

'Doing Geographicals'

The word 'geographical' comes from the recovery community. It refers to one of the actions that an alcoholic mistakenly takes in order to 'fix' their problems. It means you are changing your 'outsides' in order to fix your 'insides'. So an active alcoholic may physically move cities or jobs in the faulty belief that it is their environment that is causing the problems.

Here is the part that the loved ones of alcoholics find so hard to understand. It's easy to look at someone with a drink or drug problem and see the chaos and consequences it causes. It is therefore unbelievable to them that the alcoholic can't see it too. And that's the truth, the alcoholic *can't* see what is going on, they can't see the destruction or the impact alcohol is having. This is the insanity.

This is because the predominant thing in their lives is this constant, internal, emotional pain and dissatisfaction; this influences their choices and decisions. The constant driver is 'Will this change how I feel?' Not 'Is this going to harm me or anyone else?'.

Unfortunately, this never works, because 'wherever *you* go, there *you* are'.

This behaviour can be manifest long before the drinking becomes a serious problem, because at this point the sufferer is exploring behaviours as a method of managing their internal state, rather than just exploring substances.

The following is a common, but not exhaustive list of things an alcoholic or potential alcoholic will change in order to try and manage their internal state:

- Moving house, city or country.
- Changing jobs frequently.
- Obsessing over their appearance.
- Buying things they don't need or can't afford.
- Changing courses or studies abruptly.
- Enthusiastically starting new things but never finishing them.
- Ending relationships/marriages.

- Remarrying/getting into new relationships hastily.
- Obsessive new hobbies that peter out.

To friends and family these changes can seem bizarre and not thought through, but not necessarily a symptom of anything deeper. For the potential alcoholic the behaviour is merely an outward demonstration of how they are feeling inside. They are trying to *fix their insides by changing their outsides'* through constant activity. When eventually all these methods fail to make them happy or content, they turn to alcohol or substances to do the job.

Self-deception

This refers to the lies we tell ourselves. We all do it, from time to time, to help us cope with life. Some of the reasons we do this are to:

- Boost our ego to make ourselves look better.
- Escape punishment or judgement.
- Avoid conflict.
- Get out of something we don't want to do.
- Save (in our opinion) someone else's feelings.
- Do something that goes against our morals/beliefs.
- Secure financial advantage.
- Cover up our feelings of low self worth.

I don't believe that anyone is scrupulously honest all of the time. It would be impossible; we can only *strive* for honesty in all areas of our lives, and reflect on why we lie when we do. Because of the nature of alcoholism, it fuels the need for the alcoholic to lie, and not just to others, to themselves most of all. We are all guilty of falling into the trap of wanting to be seen in a better light, it's only human.

If you think about it, for alcoholics to continue to drink in the destructive way they do, they have to be lying to themselves. It's the only way they can keep from seeing the destruction they are causing. Alcoholics don't mean to lie to their friends and loved ones, but they are lying so much to themselves that it is almost impossible for them to be honest with anyone else. Of course, it wasn't like this from the beginning.

My story

There was a point, when I was a child, when I believed anything was possible. I may have only just been at the beginning of living a life in fear; paradoxically, I still had fearlessness. I believed I could be anything. The world was there for me to fulfil my dreams in. When I said I wanted to become a doctor, a vet, an astronaut, a movie star, be somebody, do something when I grew up, I really believed that I could.

And then as time went on, fear overtook me and I forgot what I was capable of. I withdrew inside myself, ignored my dreams, my hopes, my passions, and compromised myself. I settled for less than second best and rationalised that this was reality. I became someone I didn't recognise.

Deep in my heart, in my truest self, in my soul, I knew I wasn't living the life I was meant to be living; I knew I wasn't the person I was meant to be; I knew I was lying to myself, but I had to keep lying in order to keep doing what I was doing to myself.

The first lie was like a thin layer of tissue paper laid over my spirit (my inner voice) – no big deal, it just makes the voice a little less insistent. But then I told myself another lie. Another layer of tissue was laid over that voice to muffle it a little more, and so it goes on.

If we keep doing this, lying to ourselves, we are not becoming what we are capable of becoming. Then the layers of tissue, of lies, get thicker and thicker and the voice (our truth within us) becomes muffled and distant, to the point where we can barely hear it and we have completely forgotten anything true about ourselves. Tissue paper is easily torn and discarded, but imagine 800 layers of it melded together like paper mâché; it becomes a wall inside us. When this happens, a separation occurs inside ourselves. *We lose our voice. Our internal compass is lost. Our spirit is suffocated.* We are at the mercy of the elements. We become disconnected from *who we really are.*

"You know, most of us deny our feelings. Society has taught us to do that. From a young age, we divorce ourselves from the way we feel. We're told not to cry, we're told not to laugh too loud, and we're told that it's wrong to feel sad or even to experience our anger. But our feelings are neither right nor wrong – they are simply feelings, and an essential part of the human experience. Deny them and you begin to shut down parts of yourself. Keep doing that and you'll lose the connection to who you truly are. You'll begin living completely in your head, and you'll stop feeling." Sharma, 2002

Denying our true selves is like living life with one arm tied behind your back. It's a denial of a *part* of ourselves, *the most important part*. The part of us that is our essential truth. This is where the most unbearable pain comes from and this is why we feel we *must* anaesthetise it. This is where the drinking and other coping behaviours come in. Alcohol is a very effective anaesthetic.

The Emperor's New Clothes

Sometimes I feel like the little boy from the Hans Christian Andersen story, who stands in line to watch the emperor parade his finest robes to his subjects. The robes have been specially made by two confidence tricksters, who spin the message that the cloth is *so* special, *so* magical, *so* fine that only really clever people can see it; to anyone else it would be invisible. Of course, no one dare admit they can't see anything because they don't want to appear stupid or different from other people; they don't want to point out that there are no clothes, so they all lie and exclaim how fine the robes are. When the emperor is parading in these new robes he is actually naked but nobody dare tell him. Except for one little boy, who can't help but be honest. He points and says 'But he's not wearing any clothes!' and from that one statement the whole crowd finally has permission to see the truth and they all start laughing at the emperor's vanity and nakedness.

So I want to point at our nakedness, not the drinking: I want to point at our behaviour and the web of lies we have spun around it.

A common story

The nineteen year-old lying in her own vomit outside a bar with her group of friends shrieks in mirth as she staggers to get up, inadvertently exposing her G-string to the passing crowd of boys, who all make crude and disdainful remarks about her. But the boys, seeing her later in the club, buy her more drinks so she won't resist one of them feeling her up in the alleyway behind the disco. She can't recall the boy's name and he didn't ask for her number. She pulls down her skirt, aware that passers-by can see, and she feels fleeting shame that is quickly exting-uished by the amount of vodka she has drunk.

The boy disappears, she isn't sure how she got home or where her friends ended up. Her head is spinning as she passes out fully clothed on her bed.

The next morning she wakes with a hangover. Nothing a fry up and Bloody Mary shouldn't fix. Recollections of the night before float through her mind. Who was that boy? He wasn't even good looking. Why did she let him do those things? This time shame floods through her body and this time it doesn't leave her.

She calls her friends and 'spins' what actually happened and how she truly felt. They tell her she was 'out of it'; she tells them what an amaz-ing night she had. Her friends lie too and agree they had a 'blinding' night. "It was a scream," they said.

The nineteen year-old swallows her shame, her loss of dignity, the unworthiness she feels and she 're-frames' the night's events under the category 'good night out'; she cross references it with 'fun and excitement' and it is filed in her memory. She has created the belief, through her own spin, that her behaviour the night before adds up to a good night out.

The pattern is set. She repeats the pattern.

Who are you?

Ask yourself, "Are you who you really are?" That may seem like a strange question, but ask it anyway. If you are *not* who you are meant to be, then how do you numb the pain of that answer?

What I'm suggesting is that our culture's relationship with alcohol could have something to do with an inability to deal with these feelings. We hide and pretend, make excuses rather than face up to our truth. To be fair, we have not been taught how to deal with our inner worlds. Few of us are given the opportunity to understand our feelings and emotions and how they can limit or serve us. We react to our feelings: we fix them, keep them hidden, suppress them, deny them, and pretend everything is OK. What we *don't* do is learn how to manage them.

Because we don't ourselves understand our varying feelings, it becomes even harder to articulate them to another person. That is, of course, supposing we have another person we can trust.

My story

The first feeling I ever had was of being wrong, different, uncomfortable; my whole life experience prior to getting sober was how painful life could be. I knew something was very wrong with me; the way I felt was too terrible to try to articulate to another person, it was so arbitrary and intangible. I couldn't begin to put it into words.

Through my work I've realised that I haven't been the only one who has felt this way. I had a client who was a successful, good-looking professional man in his mid-thirties, whose marriage was breaking up. Prior to seeing me he admitted he had never let another human being in his whole life see him *as he really was.* Because he was just too frightened.

Through the therapeutic relationship we established, he was able to trust me, and he began slowly to dismantle the wall he had built around his real self. Witnessing this in a human being for the first time is like seeing a flower open. It is awe-inspiring every time. Every time. And tragic. Tragic that this walking, talking, breathing human being could walk around this world dying on the inside – everyone else around him thinking he was OK – and never having the words to ask for help. When he finally told his friends and employers he was an alcoholic and addict, they were all stunned. Nobody could believe it because he had created such a convincing 'front'. Nobody had ever taught him about how to deal with his feelings, let alone indicated to him that he even had any.

We worked together for over three years and very slowly he began to connect with and recognise his feelings. He was able to look at his past and how it had shaped him. It was a massive step for him to let someone into his internal world. It frightened him, as he had always held a deep belief that if anyone really saw what was inside him, saw who he really was, they would reject him. He was so unhappy that he finally took the risk of opening up and beginning to understand his thoughts and feelings. From that point, his behaviour began to make sense to him and he was able to start living a more authentic life.

Eventually his life turned around, he quit alcohol and drugs and he was able to establish an intimate relationship and risk revealing his true self, not the false one he had created. He is now in a committed relationship, has two young children, and his own business.

Understanding our internal worlds

Human beings are programmed to find the shortest route to fulfilment and pleasure. We look for quick fixes when we feel empty and hurt. It is easy to understand any addiction, including to food and cigarettes, within this context.

The user perceives that the chemical will change how they feel, for the better. This is perhaps also the reason why people end up eating too much, sleeping around, buying things they don't need or getting into relationships for the wrong reasons. The driving force of these behaviours is the feelings that underlie them. What we are all trying to do is to be happy and fulfilled, and any behaviour of this type is simply undertaken in the belief that it will bring happiness or satisfaction, even if it is only temporary.

Choosing to live your truth

The most profound thing that happened to me when I first got sober was the discovery that I hadn't been *'living my truth'*. I realised that each of us has a 'truth' deep inside us. It is the essence of who we are. It determines the choices we make and how we express ourselves. To my horror I realised I had become a 'fake' person. I made choices based on other people's approval, not my own. I expressed opinions I thought other people would want to hear, regardless of whether I believed them or not. I had lost my path. I saw how this was tied into my drinking, how alcohol numbed the understanding of what I was doing (because deep down I knew). So I saw for the first time that I had to begin to be true to myself if I wanted to overcome drinking.

Living your truth is hard.

Not living your truth is harder.

Make your choice.

Only one of these choices leads to completeness, peace and joy, to *freedom,* whilst the other leads to darkness and despair.

I realised I had a choice in how I lived. Up until then I had no idea that I had a choice or could control the direction of my life, but I saw that every time I chose to do or say something that was incongruent with who I was, then I was choosing not to live my truth.

I had lost myself.

Who I had become was not my truth.

That's why I hurt so much.

That's why I had to anaesthetise the hurt.

That's why I drank.

I was the emperor with no clothes, pretending that I wasn't naked, surrounded by people who colluded in my self-deception. Everything was superficial and false.

I didn't know how to communicate with anyone; I had never learnt about my 'inside world' and how much this mattered, how much it impacted on my outside world.

Nobody had ever told me about how to deal with my feelings, how to be true to myself, how to act with integrity. It's only after years of personal development and seeking answers that I have finally found what I have been looking for: *that my external world is a reflection of my internal world; if I take care of that, then everything else will be OK.*

This is the world's best kept secret.

Just think how different our lives would be if we were all true to ourselves. If we didn't feel ashamed, embarrassed or confused about how we felt. Imagine what it would be like if we were all so much more authentic.

The Emperor's New Clothes is a parable that teaches children that pride comes before a fall. Pride is bound up with what we think other people think about us. It trips us up when we place an emphasis on being happy through influencing and manipulating other people's opinion of us. If we get trapped in this illusion then we become victims of self-delusion, like the emperor.

There's something about alcohol abuse that steals our authenticity, that erodes our integrity and keeps us hypnotised by all the promises it fails to deliver. It promises us joy, companionship, connection, love, popularity, fun, excitement, but when we receive those much sought after gifts they are hollow, without worth, an empty promise, an illusion created by our own longing for it to be so.

Like the emperor's new clothes, it's a trick, a falsehood, a lie that we are all willingly buying into again and again, because it's not the fine clothes or alcohol that we actually seek, it's the *feelings* we think they will bring us.

It's the feelings we are chasing. We want to change how we feel.

Chapter 3

What drives people to drink?

Fear is the engine that drives alcoholism. In order to live with this fear the alcoholic goes into denial so they can continue drinking. However, we must learn to manage fear, as it is part of the human experience. It is how we grow. All life is dynamic. We are either growing or dying.

S O FAR W E have looked at the role alcohol has played in our culture, and the damaging effects of alcohol. We have also begun to explore the dishonesty that exists around our relationship with alcohol and how much we drink. The previous chapter introduced the significance of managing our internal world, how it impacts on our behaviour, and how this can set up the conditions that lead to alcoholism. Now it is time to look more closely at the most significant drivers leading to alcoholism:

- Fear.
- Denial.
- Emotional unmanageability.

I would argue, from what I've seen in all my work with alcoholics, that *fear* and dealing with fear are the defining factors of alcoholism. It is simply overwhelming and the alcoholic or potential alcoholic has little or no way of dealing with it.

Fear and alcoholism

Fear is a universal experience. Everybody feels fear. Very few of us talk about it.

If we do it's at a superficial level. People rarely open up about what they're really scared about, which is extraordinary, because we're all scared of more or less the same things:

- Rejection.
- Being vulnerable.
- Loneliness.
- Other people.
- Not being good enough.
- Not being loved.
- Speaking in public.
- What other people think of us.
- Someone seeing who we really are.
- Failure.
- Success.
- People laughing at us.
- Looking stupid.
- And – other people finding out we're frightened!

How many did you recognise?

There are, of course, many more, but this is an example of the core fears most people have to some degree, but are least able to speak about. I would boil these fears down two dominant ones:

- I'm not good enough, and therefore,
- I won't be loved.

It is my belief, and professional experience, that these two fears exist inside everyone at some point. It is part of the human experience. It also seems to me that potential alcoholics are the least equipped to deal with these fears. Dealing with our deepest fears is something we can learn to do at any point in our lives. Some people can deal with them very easily. Others develop healthy or unhealthy coping strategies. As a last resort, alcohol and drugs will just temporarily block out any fears of not being good enough or not being loved.

What is also true is that fears can be imagined and irrational. However, this doesn't make the experience of them feel any less real. A child can be scared of monsters under the bed. We can tell them to not be silly, we can show them there is nothing under their bed, but once that irrational fear takes hold, it can be hard to let it go.

When dealing with an alcoholic's irrational or imagined fears, it's no good telling them to 'snap out of it,' 'get over it,' or, 'not to be so silly'. In fact, it is almost irrelevant what the fear is, what is important is the way that fear is managed, not what the fear actually is. So the alcoholic has to find a healthy way of dealing with the fears that are part of the human experience. Solutions to this are offered in the second part of this book.

Fear becomes the default setting for an alcoholic. They live in fear constantly, are frightened of the world and are constantly trying to find ways of dealing with the fear. In order to understand alcoholism, we must understand how alcoholics react to fear and how it can come to dominate their lives.

Fear is such an unpleasant emotion that we want to get rid of it as quickly as possible. So we tend to choose whatever solution works the fastest. We often make the big mistake of choosing something that is ultimately destructive. However, because our need is immediate, we are unable to consider long-term consequences: if we are frightened, we want it to end NOW!

Here are some common methods of dealing with fear:
- Drinking alcohol.
- Taking drugs.
- Cigarettes.
- Overeating.
- Gambling.
- Moving jobs/house.
- Watching TV excessively.
- Meaningless sex.
- Risk taking.
- Inappropriate relationships.
- Ignoring facts.
- Doing anything not to be alone.
- Complete denial.
- Getting angry.

The truth is that we will never be free from fear. As long as we continue to grow we will experience fear. However, what we can change is how we *deal* with it so that it no longer disables us.

Susan Jeffers, in her book *Feel the Fear and Do it Anyway*, discusses how fear is a natural accompaniment to growth and therefore cannot be avoided. From the day we are born, we are growing and seeking new experiences, with those new experiences comes fear. Again, It is the *management of that fear* that is key.

For some of us, our first day of school was frightening. It was the unknown, after all, and the unknown can be frightening. We are leaving the comfort of what we know and are stepping into a world we know nothing about. We don't know what to expect and that frightens us.

I remember sobbing to my mother the night before I went to high school when I was eleven. I was terrified and overwhelmed. It was a big change and it felt like a world I wasn't ready for. I was frightened up until lunchtime on my first day and then it just became normal. I had pushed through the fear; it was the natural accompaniment to a new experience.

Some of us are frightened on our first day of a new job. Others can just take it in their stride. Learning to drive, doing a presentation at work, meeting strangers at a party, letting someone down, saying no, all these things are frightening to a lesser or greater degree to different kinds of people. We learn to cope with the situations as best we can, and as we get older and have more life experience these things become easier.

Some alcoholics can deal with certain fears quite easily and even do things normal people would balk at; they can be fearless in their behaviour at times. I've worked with extremely successful people, who have achieved great things in their professional lives. In order to do this they have had to find a way to manage their fears. So, fear can drive people to achieve great things; fear of poverty can motivate someone to amass a fortune.

But, even if they have achieved great things, every alcoholic is full of fear. For example, the chief executive of a successful company who is in a cold empty marriage because he is too frightened to open up to his wife; or the beautiful model on the cover of magazines who is frightened that no one really loves her; or the housewife with three children who is frightened of the other mothers at the school gate, because she's scared they are judging her.

Despite outside appearances, fear is dominating their lives. The chief executive comes home every night and drinks himself into a stupor. The model doesn't eat and has wine for breakfast instead. The housewife has a bottle of vodka in her bag to swig at before she picks up her kids. It is fear of the rational and irrational. Whatever the fears are, they feel very real to the person experiencing them.

Sometimes alcoholics are scared of the obvious things, such as speaking in public, meeting new people and so on, but in my experience they are more usually frightened of the hidden things: not being good enough, being a failure, not being loved.

Fear can manifest itself in many ways, and in relation to alcoholism I am referring mostly to the hidden fears: the ones that no one ever really talks about – because they're scared to. These are the disabling, all encompassing fears that drive a person to seek relief in drink.

When a person's drinking is progressing, it is the fear of how they are going to be able to *deal* with their fears that makes the thought of giving up drinking so hard. They usually haven't ever told anyone how they feel because it's almost impossible to put into words. But they are terrified, even when they know alcohol is destroying their lives; they are terrified of how they are going to deal with life without its support. They believe that alcohol is the only thing that is helping them deal with their fear.

Understanding this, and supporting the alcoholic to find new ways to deal with their fears, is an essential component to recovery from alcoholism. I believe that if the alcoholic doesn't find a better way to manage fear then they will either return to drinking or simply replace alcohol with another substance or unhealthy behaviour.

Fear is simply too overwhelming to ignore.

The Universal Law of Life

There is a Universal Law of Life. If you look around, you will see it is undeniably true: *we are either growing, or we are dying.*

Look at a plant or a tree; it is either growing or dying.

Look at an animal; it is either growing (maturing) or dying.

Look at a company or organisation; it is either growing (improving, adapting) or dying.

Look at a person; they are either growing (maturing, getting wiser) or they are dying (not growing, not learning, not getting wiser).

Do you see?

We *have* to grow, or we die.

And if we grow, then we are going to encounter fear, because growing always means encountering new experiences, and new experiences can bring fear. We just can't avoid growing. Becoming *more* (growing) is our purpose and our destiny. Our challenge is to continue to grow whilst managing the fear.

Sometimes when the fear has overwhelmed someone they stop growing, because it becomes too frightening. What happens then is that people start limiting their lives and never move out of the comfort zones. They never challenge themselves and always stay within what they know. They believe that by so doing they will avoid fear. Their lives become reduced. They don't take risks or make any changes. They exert a lot of effort in trying to control their immediate environment, believing that this will keep fear at bay. But what happens is that instead of avoiding fear they generate more of it because they are not growing, and if they are not growing then they are dying, and *nothing* is more frightening than this.

The first and most important part of dealing with fear is to admit, 'I'm frightened!'.

This can provide some relief, as it is a truthful statement of how one feels rather than the lie of denying it. Trying to deny how we really feel, or ignoring the feelings or minimising them, just enables us to stay stuck in the same uncomfortable place, searching for temporary relief. Acknowledgement of how we really feel is vital. Denying our feelings can be deadly. It can literally kill us.

So the first step is to be honest with yourself and admit your fear. Facing up to our fears is ironically much easier than we think.

I'm going to let you into a little secret that may possibly change your life. If it doesn't then it will certainly make you feel a little more comfortable:

Everyone else is frightened too! Everyone.

Whenever you're frightened because you've been pushed out of your comfort zone and you're doing something different, everyone else around you is probably feeling the same way. But because we are so used to hiding it, we look around us and think we are the only one feeling this way. In Britain, where I come from, we have this tradition of a 'stiff upper lip,' which effectively translates as, 'never, under any circumstance show how you really feel'. Now this may be a necessary policy in some situations, but more often than not it has led to our pretending *not to feel* what we actually feel. Ever.

There is only one way to deal with fear and that is to face up to it, to understand you are going to feel it, but move forward anyway; it's a paradox, the only way *over* it is *through* it.

Nobody feels fear the way alcoholics feel fear

I'm aware that's not exactly true. However, there's something about alcoholic thinking that twists all our emotions and makes the unpleasant ones dominant in us. We seem to take fear to a whole new level, much more than ordinary people do. It's like I was born frightened and my whole life has been a reaction to the fear. None of my fears were real, they were always imagined, but they seemed real to me and they followed me wherever I went. It was like a cancer of the mind, spreading and destroying everything in its path.

When I first got sober I didn't really identify with other alcoholics. I just hadn't experienced any of the things they had. I had never been arrested, divorced or bankrupt. I hadn't been caught drink driving or been homeless. None of that stuff had happened to me. I was just a stupid girl from Norfolk who drank too much and made a fool of herself.

However, when I listened to another alcoholic describe how they felt, then I knew without a doubt that I was an alcoholic too. It was the fear that they described that I related to, the fear of people, or what they thought, or what I thought they thought. I was frightened of making decisions, and paralysed with the fear of making the wrong one. I was frightened of not being good enough, and of other people finding out I wasn't good enough. I was frightened of loneliness, of not being loved, of pain, of death. I was frightened of not reaching my potential. I was frightened of the world and I was frightened of everything, anything and nothing. I couldn't put my fear into words. I was terrified of anyone seeing I was frightened. I lived with it. It was natural; my predominant experience of living life up until I got sober was dealing with fear on one level or another. I didn't know there was any other way to experience being in this world.

A common story continued

The nineteen year-old begins to feel anxious when she goes into college on Monday. Everyone is laughing about how she behaved on Saturday night. She laughs too, but can't shake the feeling that they are laughing at her rather than with her. She feels confused. She thought she was just like everyone else, except that she doesn't feel right inside despite her 'couldn't care less' attitude. A knot of anxiety develops in her stomach and doesn't leave.

She doesn't understand herself any more. She feels like she is a good person, a considerate person and yet she has behaved terribly to one of her friends. A couple of them are barely speaking to her because of stuff she said when she was drunk. She doesn't remember, but she feels frightened every time she sees them. She doesn't know if they like her any more and that frightens her. These fears creep in and take up residence in her mind. They are never quiet, always nagging at her. Someone asks her if she is 'all right?' She says, 'of course,' because she doesn't know how to put words to the darkness spreading through her mind. It's better to close it off, push it away, pretend it doesn't exist. For brief periods she can forget she's afraid of anything. She looks forward to those periods more and more.

She's going out again this Friday, and Saturday, and probably Sunday as well. It's something to look forward to. It takes her mind off things.

Fear very nearly killed me. It manifested itself as panic attacks that went on for nearly ten years, almost on a daily basis. Panic attacks are very common in alcoholics or binge drinkers. They are fear manifested in an extremely frightening and disabling way. Because alcohol is a depressant*, it can cause feelings of anxiety and not being able to cope. Abuse of alcohol interferes with the brain chemistry and can result in feelings of anxiety. Combine this with the feelings of fear that were already there and alcohol just exacerbates the problem. What often happens is that the individual will then use more alcohol to cope with these feelings, or look for other means, such as prescription or illegal drugs.

My story

My fear crippled me. I lived in blind terror every day. Everything was frightening for me. Other people terrified me. I felt so worthless in their eyes and was sure they would see any minute what a despicable human being I was and discard me. At any given time I couldn't really explain what I was frightened of. I just knew that I was scared. It ate me up inside. I would try to act as if it wasn't there, try to ignore it, but it would come back stronger.

Some days it felt like I could barely breathe because the fear was crushing me. It made me feel sick. I struggled to find different ways to cope with it. Drink, of course, numbed it briefly. I tried to ask for help, but I couldn't find the words that would make someone take me seriously. I wanted to be saved. I wanted someone to pick me up and put me in a nice padded room and tell me I would never have to worry about anything ever again. I wanted to go mad, but I was too frightened to, so I just stayed in this perpetual state of unqualified fear.

The role of denial in alcoholism

Denial = how we lie to ourselves.

Denial is a psychological defence mechanism that prevents the alcoholic from seeing the truth of what they are doing to themselves. It prevents them from becoming aware of what alcoholism is costing them and therefore

---

* *"Almost all drinkers seeking help report symptoms of anxiety and depression. Alcohol is a depressant drug. Prolonged drinking can lead to profound and long lasting mood swings. Symptoms of alcohol-induced depression can be severe but subside during abstinence."* Alcohol Concern Factsheet: Alcohol and Mental Health, 2002

blocks any growing anxiety they would feel. So whilst they are avoiding the uncomfortable feelings of anxiety, they are also avoiding reality.

Denial is a big part of the problem; denial is when we continue to drink to the extent that we are harming ourselves and refuse to see that this is the case. The alcoholic has tunnel vision and disregards the disturbing reality of what is actually happening in their lives. Denial is what prevents the alcoholic from doing anything about their problem. Once we realise there is a problem there is a strong urge to do something about it. But when the alcoholic is faced with the idea of not drinking it is extremely frightening to them, as they don't know how they will cope without it. So the spiral of fear, denial and more drinking continues.

Denial is a form of self-deception. A person in denial has *selective* perception. They will only see what they allow themselves to see. Denial is when we lie to ourselves. Denial causes much internal distress.

Denial can manifest itself in many different forms:

- **Minimising**
  - When an alcoholic minimises their drinking they are aiming to give the impression that they are drinking far less than it appears. They may say they only had two or three drinks last night when it's true they did have two or three glasses, but each glass held half a bottle of wine!

- **Rationalising**
  - This is the process we go through when we try to justify unjustifiable events with a plausible story; we are 'spinning' what actually happened. When you rationalise, you always look to blame outside factors for why you drink the way you do. Alcoholics will often blame others or outside circumstances to rationalise their behaviour.

- **Blaming**
  - When we don't want to take responsibility for ourselves we blame our past or present for why we drink so much, or the people in our lives, or our circumstances or environment. When we blame, we want something other than ourselves to be the cause of the alcohol problem:
    - 'I was abused as a child.'
    - 'My partner doesn't understand me.'

- 'The police are out to get me.'
- 'I hate my job, but I can't leave it.'

- **Hostility**
  - This is when someone is openly aggressive, hostile and angry every time the subject of their drinking behaviour comes up. Usually they cause a fight and intimidate the other person so that they become too scared to bring it up again. This is exactly what the alcoholic wants. Hostility is a defence mechanism, as the people around you will know that if they say anything to you that you don't like you will get angry. This frightens most people, so it prevents people from being honest with you.

Denial is how we lie to ourselves to continue doing what destroys us.

Breaking down denial is key to an alcoholic's changing. It must be noted that these psychological defence mechanisms operate unconsciously to protect the user from the painful realisation of what their drinking is doing. Sometimes just hearing another alcoholic tell their story is enough for some alcoholics to identify and realise that all this time they have been deceiving themselves. Others need professional therapeutic help so that the reality of their situation can be revealed to them in a way that doesn't harm them.

Denial is a major characteristic of alcoholism and the power of it cannot be underestimated. Remember, when an alcoholic is still in the grip of alcoholism they will find a way of justifying their drinking in any way they can. Denial is warped thinking; in their *right minds* the alcoholic would never jeopardise their homes, jobs, finances, health, future or children. But the powerful urge to drink overrules all of these considerations, because the need to numb their emotional pain through drink will always win. This is aided and abetted by the power of their denial.

Unmanageability

As drinking progresses it inevitably impacts our lives negatively; it causes us to be unreliable, thoughtless, inconsiderate and unable to manage our own lives.

In the 12 Steps of Alcoholics Anonymous, the first step states:

"Step One: We admitted we were powerless over alcohol - that our lives had become unmanageable." The Big Book of Alcoholics Anonymous, Fourth edition, 2001.

Within the AA programme, this is the first step the alcoholic needs to take, which is a step towards self-honesty. It is where the alcoholic takes a cold, hard look at the consequences of their drinking and for the first time admits there is a problem. The 12 steps of AA are used in treatment clinics the world over, and initially when a client comes into treatment they are introduced to this first step. They are invited to look, sometimes for the first time, at the destruction their drinking has caused in their own lives and the lives of people they love. This is one of the ways that the denial is broken down.

The unmanageability of alcoholism can present itself in numerous ways:

- Unpaid bills
- Debt
- Broken relationships
- Broken promises
- Drink driving
- Criminal charges
- Fraud
- Neglect of children
- Neglect of self
- Unexplained accidents
- Loss of personal possessions
- Problems at work
- Getting fired from jobs
- Leaving jobs before getting fired
- Disorganisation
- Losing things
- Physical injury
- Bad timekeeping
- Memory loss
- Homelessness
- Violence.

The list is really endless. The bottom line is that when someone is drinking alcohol to excess their lives become chaotic. They can't stay on top of things. They can't keep commitments. They are consistently unreliable. As their drinking progresses, the consequences usually become more serious.

I had one client who, when he first came to see me, was married with two children. He owned a large house and had a good job. He knew he had a problem with drinking, but didn't want to give it up. He didn't think it was 'that bad yet'. He believed that the problems in his life were due to his not liking his job. So he carried on drinking. One by one, all the things that mattered went: his wife kicked him out; he lost his job; he got another one and lost that too. He got caught drink driving and lost his licence. He threatened his wife when drunk and she got an injunction and then he couldn't see his kids. He got kicked out of the shared flat he was renting and ended up in a homeless shelter. No member of his family was speaking to him. He had no friends. He is still trying to get sober. It was tragic watching him lose everything that mattered. If this isn't an example of progressive unmanageability, I don't know what is. He couldn't manage his own life. The reason he could never get sober is that he couldn't face up to the fact that alcohol was causing all of his problems. He blamed everyone and everything around him.

Emotional Unmanageability

But there is also another level of unmanageability, and that is *emotional unmanageability.* To some degree, the alcoholic may be able to create some sense of order in their outside world. They may be able to work and pay their mortgage, for instance. This is how some alcoholics can convince themselves they don't have a problem; because they have a job and a car they believe things can't be that bad. However, their emotional life is completely unmanageable, and by that I mean *they have no control over how they are going to feel.* Using alcohol gives them the false illusion that they have control over their feelings, when the opposite is actually true.

They succumb to depression and irritability; they have a constant feeling of dissatisfaction. They get angry over small issues; they constantly resent other people for what they do or say. They are unhappy. Small things upset them and they over-react.

Emotional unmanageability is when you have no control over how you are going to feel or react at any particular time.

If you have no control over how you feel, then your feelings lead you, and you become a slave to them. Being in charge of your emotional life, rather than the other way round, is essential to long term recovery. (See Chapter 7: Internal navigation systems and how to use them.)

We behave how we feel

Everyone, whether or not they are alcoholics, has positive and negative feelings and then acts upon those feelings. All behaviour is dictated by how we feel; we act emotionally. We may think we make rational decisions but how we feel always takes precedence. Just look around and you will see that this is true. Now here is the catch: if your emotions are unmanageable, and you have no control over when or why you feel negative emotions, then these emotions will dictate how you behave. This is because when we feel bad we are motivated to get rid of that feeling as quickly and as effectively as possible. And alcohol is a powerful anaesthetic for negative emotions.

Now, when something bad happens it is appropriate to feel sad, disappointed, upset and so on about whatever the event was. If we lose something or someone we love it is appropriate to feel sad and to grieve, not pleasant perhaps, but necessary so that we can eventually accept that person's death and move on when the time is right. If you lose out on a promotion at work it is appropriate to feel disappointed and upset, maybe even angry, but then it is necessary to use those feelings to self-reflect, learn the lessons required and move on, applying what you have learnt.

Every day we are presented with new opportunities to grow, learn and develop. Everybody experiences ups and downs in their lives; these experiences and how we choose to respond to them are what enables us to become better versions of ourselves. Our feelings about these up and down events are a key factor in our learning and growth experiences. If we do not take advantage of the learning opportunities, then we are doomed to repeat the same mistakes over and over again. We get stuck, don't grow and that becomes painful. We start having negative feelings for no apparent reason. We don't know what our feelings mean or how to change them in a positive and effective manner. This is emotional unmanageability. It doesn't have to be like this.

The behaviour of an alcoholic makes sense to them at the time

So, with some understanding of how alcoholics really feel and what is actually motivating them, it becomes easier to understand why alcoholics behave they way they do.

From the outside an alcoholic's behaviour can seem to be that of a lunatic. I can assure you, *to them*, at the time, their behaviour makes perfect sense – because it is based on how they feel. One of the worst things about a descent into alcoholism is the realisation that you are behaving in a way that isn't *you.*

My experience as a therapist is that when the alcoholic begins to lie to himself or herself and to other people, this is when it becomes painful to be *who they are,* and this is when an alcoholic starts to drink even more to deal with these feelings.

This is when things start to spiral out of control: when alcohol stops being the solution and starts becoming the problem. *This is when it becomes impossible to stop...without help.*

PART 3

THE SOLUTION

Chapter 4

Getting the help you need

Putting down the drink and getting expert help is the first step. Explore what options are right for you. Help is needed but the solution ultimately is inside yourself. Take things slowly.

N OW FOR THE good news. Recovery from alcoholism is entirely possible. Legions of people the world over can attest to this.

Even better news? Recovery from alcoholism is not only possible, but affords a much better life as a result. How's that for starters?

If you've got this far and decided you *might* be an alcoholic, or care about someone who might be an alcoholic, then you're probably interested in what to do next.

In this chapter we are going to look at the solution, and what is required to start *living in the solution*, rather than living in the problem.

We are going to look at how to stop drinking and what help you can get, as well as what work needs to be done in order to establish long term sobriety.

Understanding what the problem is, and what the problem isn't

In order to understand what the solution is we have to clearly understand what it *isn't*.

Clients come to me because they have a problem. Usually the problem is that they don't feel good and they will have lots of reasons why that is. Often they focus on their work situation, or relationship, or lack of money, or people just not doing what they should be doing. If only all these things would change then *they* would feel OK – surely?

Afraid not.

It's not the outside world that needs to change – it's you and only you. The way it works is this: if I am OK, the world is OK. It *doesn't work* the other way round. Tough?

Let me be crystal clear here. The problem *isn't* your:

- Circumstances
- Relationship
- Weight
- Job
- Friends
- Lack of money
- Parents
- Children
- Or anything else outside of yourself.

The problem is how you *deal* with these issues, how you *see* them and how you *react* to them.

A common mistake is to believe that the problem is where you're living or working and that, if you change that situation, then everything will be OK; this is called 'doing a geographical'. Clients commonly tell me they're thinking of completely changing their circumstances because they're stuck and in a rut. All you achieve by doing this is to take yourself with you.

Wherever you go, there you are, no matter how fast or how far you run or whatever externals you change.

Because you take *yourself* with you – the same thinking, the same way of seeing the world – then inevitably you will get the same consequences.

Lifestyle changes *might* work for a short period of time, but inevitably the person just reverts to type, creating the same problems and the same unsatisfactory experiences wherever they go, whatever they do. They have made changes, but they haven't *progressed*.

Because alcoholism is so misunderstood, most people don't focus on their drinking as being the problem. I've had clients who visited doctors and alcohol professionals and who were told that they didn't drink enough to have a problem! Many professionals look at the external factors and make evaluations based on these. Some alcoholics, who have had years of problem drinking, are still being convinced they can 'learn' how to drink half a bottle of wine instead of the whole bottle.

This is the delusion of alcoholism.

So it's time to stop blaming everything around you and start taking responsibility for how your life has turned out. The first step to take is actually to stop drinking: complete total sobriety – no alcohol whatsoever.

When you have finally made the immensely important and brave decision, you need to get some help. Remember three things here:

- It's a brave person who asks for help, not a weak one.
- Doing things your way hasn't worked.
- Get help. It's important to get the help that is right for you, and to understand the significance of not doing this on your own.

There comes a point when we can't trust our own thinking or perspective on our condition, so we need other people to help us. This is the case for everyone. Sometimes we just can't see a way out of the forest, so we need a guide. I think every client who has ever come to see me has tried unsuccessfully (sometimes for years) to manage things on their own, and failed miserably. You need to seek experienced and/or professional help in order to get sober and stay sober.

A WORD OF CAUTION

If you are alcohol *dependent,* meaning you are physically dependent on alcohol, then it is extremely unsafe for you to stop drinking without a medical intervention of some kind. Alcohol is far more dangerous to detox from than say, heroin, because the sufferer could die if not properly supported (this isn't necessarily the case with a heroin detox; it's extremely unpleasant, but not usually dangerous if managed). It is very, very, important if you are a regular, heavy drinker that you seek medical help if you want to stop.

You can do this in many ways. The first step would be to go and see your doctor. You can then be referred to a local specialist service, or be prescribed medication that will enable you to detox from alcohol safely. Your doctor should be the best resource for what support and treatment are available to you locally. If you are in bad physical shape then it may be appropriate that you enter an in-patient facility where you will receive full medical care. This is to prevent withdrawal symptoms like seizures, restlessness and arrhythmia from becoming life threatening. It can also help relieve the symptoms of anxiety, restlessness and insomnia that often accompany the first few days of alcohol withdrawal. *It is essential you seek professional medical help that can assess what is the best option for you.*

If you have come to the decision that you are going to get help and stop drinking, then enlist support and help from your friends and family. I can assure you they will be relieved and happy that you have finally admitted there is a problem. Most of them will want to help.

We can kid ourselves for a long time that no one knows about our drinking or how bad it is: the truth is, it's probably been obvious for a long time. Or you may feel ashamed or embarrassed, that people may judge you or think you're weak. This is also nonsense. *You are incredibly brave.* Admitting you have a problem takes enormous courage and in many ways can be the hardest step on the road to recovery. You will feel relieved once you have done it and may be amazed at how much support is available to you.

Most people are incredibly supportive when given the chance, and instead of being judged you may find you have their respect. Everyone has problems; no one is perfect. We have all made mistakes. Most people will relate to this rather than condemn.

Other sources of help

Both the USA and the UK have an array of professional and self-help programmes. Alcoholics Anonymous is a self-funded anonymous programme and should be the first port of call for anyone struggling with a drink problem. They have over seventy years experience in dealing with alcoholics, and the programme is predicated on alcoholics helping other alcoholics. Meetings take place all over the world, so the chances are there's a free resource on your doorstep.

In addition, there are treatment centres that run residential or day programmes. Residential centres are usually based on the client establishing abstinence whilst in the programme, and looking at the deeper issues surrounding their drink or drug problem. Most of these centres, but not all, are based on the 12-step programme of Alcoholics Anonymous, and require clients to go to meetings. There are alternatives to the 12-step treatment that also require abstinence, based on Cognitive Behavioural Therapy, or other forms of holistic treatment. Whatever clinic you approach, it is a good idea to establish what their success rates are, particularly for how long clients have stayed sober after leaving their programme.

There are also a wide variety of day programmes, and specialist counsellors and practitioners of all kinds, who can advise you on what services are available locally.

Services can vary radically depending on where you live so I would advise you to do some research first. Always choose a service or professional that is qualified and accredited.

Alcoholics Anonymous

Alcoholics Anonymous (AA) is a self-help programme based on one sober alcoholic helping another alcoholic to get sober. Self-help programmes can be successful because there is an emphasis on shared experience, personal responsibility, self-motivation and a commitment to change.

AA 'meetings' take place every day, all over the world. You can find information on where your local meetings are and attend whenever you like. There is no fee or payment, just a 'pot' that is passed around at the end of the meeting for contributions towards room rent, tea and coffee.

Meetings can vary greatly depending on which ones you go to, as there is no standard format. But there is generally a secretary who opens the meeting, and different members of the group then talk about their experiences with alcohol and getting sober. The Twelve Steps of AA are usually referred to as the requirements for getting and staying sober. It is also suggested you get a 'sponsor', who is someone who has got sober through the programme and can act as your 'guide' through the process.

Alcoholics Anonymous isn't for everyone, but it can provide a supportive environment if you are first embarking on getting sober, particularly if you have no one else to support you. AA members have all gone through similar experiences and understand the impact alcohol can have. Nobody in AA will judge you.

AA – a short history

Two hopeless alcoholics who couldn't get sober developed the 12-step programme out of the principles of the Oxford Group, a religious organisation, that at the turn of the 19th century tried to help alcoholics through a basic spiritual programme. These two desperate alcoholics took the Oxford Group concepts and developed the AA 12-step programme that is based on spiritual principles that have existed through the centuries.

They took the religious aspect out, believing it to be a barrier to entry for some people, and encouraged each individual to discover their own conception of God, or a 'Higher Power' as it is often referred to.

The 12-steps can be seen as a 'toolkit' for dealing with the kind of thinking and feelings explored in this book. They deal with the underlying issues of alcoholism as we have been exploring them. The 12-steps get to the heart of the problem and give the alcoholic a new way of living, a spiritual way of living rather than a self-destructive way of living. The emphasis of the 12-steps is on a 'spiritual experience'; this is very loosely defined and AA leaves it up to its members to define what that means for each individual. What is significant is that AA recognised seventy-five years ago that alcoholism had its roots in an *internal condition of the spirit,* rather than a problem of willpower or moral fibre. A recovery movement has sprung up around this concept and is the model that is used in most treatment centres.

Further information is available at www.aa.org

How to help someone who doesn't want to stop drinking

We have discussed so far what kind of help is available for someone who is ready and wants to stop drinking. But what if you are reading this book because you care about someone who is drinking themselves to destruction and isn't ready to stop? It is terrible to watch someone drink themselves to death, lose everything and still deny there is a problem or that they need any help. We can beg, plead, threaten, but often this gets us nowhere. There is, however, something you can do. It's pretty drastic, but sometimes when we have no choices left we have to take drastic measures.

Interventions

Interventions are still relatively new in the UK. However, they are very common in the USA. There is even an acclaimed reality television show that follows families as they facilitate a professional intervention of a loved one. It has proved to be very educational for families who have a member suffering from alcoholism. Instead of a family waiting until the alcoholic realises they have reached 'rock bottom', they conduct an intervention in order to bring the alcoholic to their senses. Remember, one of the defining characteristics of alcoholism is denial, and the lies alcoholics tell themselves. They can't see reality. Instead of standing by and watching someone they love destroy themselves, the family can do something about it.

Interventions should always be facilitated by a professional, never attempt to do it by yourself. Because of the emotional involvement you have with the alcoholic, it would be very unlikely to succeed and could make things worse. Although this is a small field, it is growing. Interventions are carried out by qualified addictions therapists, who usually have personal experience of alcoholism themselves and therefore have a unique ability to 'reach' the alcoholic.

An intervention should always be thoroughly planned in advance. It should involve as many people as possible that are close to the alcoholic and have been affected by their drinking. The interventionist will very likely ask everyone to write the alcoholic a letter that explains how much they love and care about the alcoholic, and then goes on to explain how their drinking affects them and how they can't continue being in a relationship with them if they don't do something about this. The key here is to have a 'bottom line'. There have to be consequences if the alcoholic does not get help.

The alcoholic is then invited – under some guise – to a meeting, and everyone reads out their letters to the alcoholic. The facilitator will support the loved ones and ensure that the alcoholic understands they aren't being judged or blamed, but instead are just very sick and need help. This is the definition of 'tough love'. Brutal honesty, in a loving way, is what is required. The letter writing is very significant as it enables the reader to say what is important and why they love the alcoholic. It's much easier to read something than remember it off the top of your head when in a highly charged emotional environment. The more people of significance to the alcoholic who are involved, the better. The alcoholic may try to dismiss the pleas of their spouse and parent, but it becomes harder to ignore if their friends, colleagues, siblings, cousins, aunts and uncles are also saying the same thing.

The objective is to give the alcoholic nowhere to run, so their only choice is to get help. For maximum effectiveness, the alcoholic is asked to agree there and then to go into a treatment programme. They then literally pack a bag and go. If the alcoholic refuses to go into a treatment programme, then the family must be prepared to follow through on their decision, which is not to engage in a relationship with the alcoholic until they decide to get sober. This is very tough to do, but it is essential that the alcoholic understand that there are consequences to their drinking.

You can see why planning is key. A lot of organisation is required here. If you have come to the point where you believe this is the only option to help a loved one, then I would urge you to use a qualified and experienced interventionist. Ask them about their experience and what their success rate has been.

What is abstinence?

Abstinence from alcohol means not drinking at all. Ever. In any circumstances. For any reason. Yep, not even at Christmas or on birthdays.

Yes, I know, if you are only *contemplating* quitting drinking at this point then you may have just run screaming from the room. Because the thought of not drinking ever is probably the most terrifying thing you have ever heard. It can feel that way at the beginning. It does get easier, then it becomes normal, and then the very thought of drinking becomes revolting.

It is therefore important we explore this subject and what it means. It has been well established in the private treatment sector that recovery from alcoholism requires one to be abstinent. One of the defining characteristics of alcoholism is a loss of control over when, how much, and for how long you drink. Of course every alcoholic wants to believe that he or she will be the one who can learn to drink '*normally*' again.

If, at this point, you still feel that your problem with alcohol is not that serious and abstinence seems too drastic, then I would suggest you experiment with 'controlled drinking', which means this: decide how much you are going to drink and how frequently, and then see if you can stick to it. Try it for a few weeks and see what happens. If you find you are able to control your drinking without any thought or problem, then well done. If not, then don't despair, there is a solution and it's not the end of the world.

As discussed in previous chapters, drinking is ubiquitous in western culture. Our social and recreation time is built around it and it is hugely prominent in celebrations and for marking occasions. Alcohol is everywhere. It is encouraged and celebrated. So giving up alcohol can seem to be quite a challenge at first.

Abstinence from alcohol is unfortunately seen as a radical thing to do in many quarters. In fact, people often seem *scared* of it and see it as a last resort. There is an implication that living a life of abstinence could be *so bad* that anything would be better than that! If this is the case for you, then alcohol has become an obsession. Think about it. What is something else you really like? For me, it's shellfish. If I was told, for health reasons, I could never eat these again, I wouldn't necessarily be best pleased, but it wouldn't preoccupy my thoughts. I would just stop eating them.

Well it's the same with alcohol; if you suffer uselessness, belligerence, apathy, recklessness or depression because of taking alcohol, then you should stop drinking alcohol as it is clearly interfering with your ability to live fully.

I have a dear friend who has been sober for over twenty years, who tells me that when he was drinking, his wife would despair of him, threaten to leave, threaten to throw him out, beg him to stop drinking; she cried and ranted and raved at how much misery his drinking was causing the family. When he finally admitted he had a problem and wanted to stop drinking altogether his wife replied, "That's a bit drastic isn't it?".

What we have is a misconception regarding abstinence; we believe it will be dreadful.

Nothing could be further from the truth.

When your body and mind are free from chemicals and you are doing the necessary work to recover your mind, body and soul from the tyranny of alcoholism, then you can enter into a way of life that can be better than anything you could have imagined before.

A story of survival and hope

I'm including the story here of a friend of mine; she has been sober since 2006. I wanted to include her story in this book because it is typical in so many ways of the progression of alcoholism, and it illustrates all of the other issues that can compound the problem. Sobriety was the only answer for her, not controlled drinking. Once she was sober she could then begin to heal her spirit that had been so damaged by the terrible things that had been done to her, and the terrible things she then continued to do to herself. Ultimately, her story is one of survival, hope, courage and transformation. Vanessa meets people from her past who physically do not recognise her because she has changed so much on the *inside*.

Vanessa's story

I am the youngest of five girls, born and brought up on the south coast of England. At playgroup, I had three close friends, but even at that age I can remember feeling like something separated me from them. I was happiest when I was on my own, yet I craved a sense of belonging.

At age nine, my friends and I started going to different schools. I no longer had my human shield to defend me. I was fat and shy, and soon became a target for bullying on the school bus. The sense of isolation from the world grew. One day, I confided in the guy who owned the horses I used to ride. He took his opportunity, and started abusing me. I was trapped. I couldn't tell my parents, since I felt responsible for what was happening and was bizarrely under the impression that they would be angry that I might become pregnant.

The abuse carried on for three years. I remember the February night John's wife found out what was happening in the stables. She screamed at him, hit him and told me to leave.

I was alone, standing by the side of the road in the winter cold, still numb, still confused and unsure of what to do next. Then I had a single thought, which ruled my life for the next twenty-odd years: "I'll show you.". I'd show everyone – adults, children, whoever – that I didn't need them to run my life. I was going to do it my way.

At some point, I think I was fifteen, I started going out on a Friday night to a pub with a friend. I found I had a talent for drinking and that it gave me the ability to be funny, daring and confident. I felt like I thought everyone else felt all of the time. I felt like I had the code to life that I'd been missing, the thing that finally connected me with other people. At that time, just knowing that was enough, I felt like I was in on the secret.

I went to University in East Anglia to study Biochemistry. I joined the 'Crawl Club', which involved spending Friday nights doing a pub crawl, stopping at each one on the route for one drink. The following Spring I met my husband, Justin. By now, I was drinking heavily whenever I went out, and was unable to control what or how much I drank once I'd started. I don't know when I crossed the line from being a heavy binge drinker to someone who drank whatever they could whenever it was available.

The following year, Justin and I got married, and I qualified as an osteopath. A week after I got my registration, a local osteopath phoned and offered me my dream job. I started working for her, and it very quickly became obvious that either the job or the drink had to go; I couldn't do both. I also realised that everything I wanted in life – to live a long, happy life with Justin – was unattainable while I was drinking. I both loved and loathed alcohol. I was waking up wishing I were dead, chaotically getting myself into work, lasting the day promising myself I wouldn't drink, but knowing that on my way home I'd be in one of the three local shops buying a bottle of wine. By the beginning of January 2006, the depression worsened. I didn't want to die but I didn't want to live as I was. On 9 January I got help, and started to get hope.

After six weeks, I relapsed. We were going out for a Valentine's meal, and I just decided to drink. It was that simple. As soon as I opened the can of Stella, I felt different. I had two while I was getting ready. We went to a restaurant, and had oysters and champagne, plus more booze. Afterwards, we went to a pub, and when closing time came, I wanted to walk across town to another pub that did lock-ins. Justin pulled the plug and took me home. We still had some Christmas booze in the house, and again I begged him to get me more drink. He realised that I really did have a problem and chucked it all away.

The next day was horrendous. I was meant to be going to a conference, but had to phone and lie to my boss, saying I had a migraine. I didn't get out of bed for the rest of the day, and could barely move or drink water. More than anything, I felt stupid. Stupid for throwing away six weeks of sobriety and for thinking for a second that I could drink normally.

Since then, life has completely changed. Writing this today, I remember and feel all the things I've described, but I can't quite believe I am living in the same lifetime. A couple of months before I got sober, I almost drowned, and had to make the conscious decision to save my own life. I believe now that that was a kind of physical rebirth. My spiritual and emotional rebirth started with putting down the drink for good and getting help.

Vanessa 39, sober since 2004

Vanessa had many compounding problems: she was sexually abused and suffered from an eating disorder. At first glance you could assume that the sexual abuse triggered her alcoholism, but it's clear from her story that the feelings and thinking that preceded alcoholism were already active when she was five years old. What stands out the most is how amazing she feels sober, how rewarding it is. This is the truth: if life without alcohol didn't have its rewards, if it wasn't better, *significantly better* than life with alcohol, no one would be sober.

Why just stopping drinking is not enough

Just stopping drinking isn't enough. We have been exploring the underlying reasons that have caused alcoholism. When someone gets sober, those underlying issues will still be there. In fact they may be more prominent once the alcohol is removed. The 'hole in the soul' will still be there and it will need attention. What I have been trying to spell out in this book is that you can't ignore what's inside you.

There are many ways to address this, varying from professional treatment, therapy, self-help books, steps and personal development workshops. But, you must do something. *No change means no change.* Because if you don't do something, the spiritual un-wellness will either take you right back to drink in order to treat the 'hole in the soul' that is still burning, or it will manifest itself in other addictive behaviours.

We call this cross addiction, or poly-drug addiction. It means that once you are addicted to one substance you can be addicted to all. Falling into this is a common mistake people make. They recognise they have a drinking problem and manage to stop. But then the emotions and feelings they always had, that they used alcohol to escape from, are still there, and they are forced to find other chemicals or behaviours to deal with them.

If this happens, all the alcoholic has done is to replace one chemical or behaviour for another, while still running away from the root of the problem.

This is because, despite the differences in the effects of various substances, they all activate the 'pleasure centre' of the brain (Doweiko, 2012). So it doesn't matter if it's a different chemical – alcohol, cannabis, Valium – they all impact the same nerve pathways in the brain.

To demonstrate this further, research (Moorehead & Alexander, 2007) is now suggesting that obese gastric band patients are susceptible to 'addiction transference'. A gastric band shrinks your stomach to the size of a walnut, making it almost impossible to overeat. However, what doctors are discovering is that many gastric band patients are then developing addictions to alcohol or other substances. This is because they have not dealt with the underlying psychological issues that led to their overeating in the first place. Overeating and food were symptoms, like alcohol and drunkenness are symptoms; they are not, however the root of the problem.

I'm using this as an example as it effectively demonstrates that, like Prohibition, just removing the substance (for instance the ability to over-eat) that is causing the problem isn't enough. It's the beginning, and must be followed by therapeutic interventions that address the underlying causes that led to the addiction in the first place.

This can, admittedly, sound frightening, as we have established that in many ways this is what the alcoholic has been running away from all this time. It's finally time to see what is really inside us: *who we really are*. Covered in a lot of rubbish, certainly, but the essence of *who we really are* is amazing. I promise you that if you take the journey to see *who you really are*, you will be amazed and delighted.

Do you dare? If you've read this far, you probably can't afford not to. Try it. You've got nothing to lose, and, if it's not for you, you can go back to your misery. Deal?

So pack your bags, we're taking a trip....

Chapter 5

The early stages of recovery from alcoholism

Go easy on yourself. Be kind to yourself. Your mind and body are healing – saying goodbye to alcohol and hello to freedom. Learn to navigate this world slowly and at your own pace, particularly when you have to deal with friends who drink.

THIS CHAPTER IS going to explore the early stages of recovery. What is life like without alcohol? How does one live without it? These are really important questions for the recently sober alcoholic.

Alcohol has often been the best friend of the alcoholic and they have to choose to live life without it. The first few months of sobriety can feel like the hardest because everything is so new. There is a period of adjustment where the alcoholic learns how to live sober. This can include social situations, celebrations, birthdays, weekends, holidays – situations where they used to drink, but now have to navigate without the aid of drink. The first challenge may be just getting through a weekend sober. There is no hard and fast rule here for anyone, as everyone will progress at their own pace and find some situations easier to handle than others.

A good suggestion is to keep a 'dry' house for the first few months, meaning no alcohol at all in the home. Obvious drinking situations like bars, pubs and nightclubs should probably be avoided in the first few months also. These are only temporary measures and it should be stressed that once an alcoholic has a firm hold on sobriety, situations that seemed impossible before become easier and easier. Eventually, a whole new life emerges, a social life that is full and interesting without the aid of alcohol. Most recovered alcoholics comment on how full and exciting their lives are now compared to when they drank. A new life without alcohol is not empty, boring or glum, as many people fear. It is actually just the opposite.

Welcome to your new life.

What to expect in early recovery

The following is meant as a guide to support you in your early weeks of recovery from alcoholism. The first few days and weeks without alcohol can be frightening and confusing; you have, of course, put down your security blanket, your crutch, your way of coping with the world. It can be very challenging initially to go about your daily life without it.

The following are simple suggestions that when applied will greatly enhance your chances of a successful recovery; it's the small things that can sometimes make the biggest difference.

Be good to yourself. Making the decision to ask for help is an act of courage and self-love. Don't beat yourself up about the past. This will get sorted out in time. Instead, try to take each day one at a time, or just a few hours at a time and acknowledge to yourself that things can be different now and the person who drank and used drugs wasn't the real you. You only have to deal with the 24 hours in front of you. Nothing else matters right now.

Stay away from the first drink. If you don't have the first one you won't have the rest. Accept that you do not have control over alcohol and that now is the time to do things differently. If you have a craving think it through:

- What usually happens when you pick up a drink? What are the consequences?
- How do you end up feeling?
- What happens the next morning?

Make a decision that 'just for today' you won't pick up a drink. Plan your day around this thought, with actions that will support and strengthen it.

Only deal with what is right in front of you, with what is absolutely necessary. It's very easy to get sidetracked and start panicking about all the things or people that need your attention. Allow yourself the time and space you need in order to get well. Ask yourself 'Will the world end?' if I don't do this task, or see that person now? In most cases the world will keep turning just fine without you. Part of our problem is that we believe we need to be in control at all times, that things won't be OK if we don't have an input. This just isn't the case. If you have friends or family offering their help and assistance, take it.

Try to rest as much as possible. You may have difficulty sleeping. This is very common at first, and with time people's sleeping patterns generally return to normal. There are lots of things you can do to help this, besides taking medication. Investigate meditation, yoga, herbal remedies, relaxation CDs, changing your diet, exercising more and so on. You may feel drained emotionally; you might experience new feelings bubbling to the surface. Rest whenever you need to. Remember, you are healing.

Diet and exercise are key to our wellbeing. Up to now, you may have neglected yourself and will no doubt be feeling the effects of this. What we put in our bodies is our lifeblood; if you have been feeding it takeaways and booze, your body won't be running as well as it can. Start by making *small* changes that you can cope with. Don't expect to turn into Mr or Ms Fitness overnight! You may notice a craving for sweet things. Again, this is very common due to the amount of sugar your body has been consuming in alcoholic drinks. Sugar also releases a chemical high that your body has been used to getting from alcohol. At first it may be necessary to allow yourself sweet things when you have a craving, as your body needs time to adjust, but where possible try to reach for fruit rather than chocolate. Look at your diet and try to include fruit and vegetables, and have regular meals instead of picking at food or bingeing. Try moderate exercise every other day; walking for fifteen minutes a day is a good place to start. The key now is everything in moderation – except alcohol, of course! There are numerous studies that show how beneficial exercise is for our state of mind. Just do what you're capable of at the moment.

Change your routines – our brain works as a trigger. You may not think you are craving a drink or drug, but walking past your local pub or even just getting cash out of a machine can trigger automatic thoughts of drinking or using drugs, so we end up following through before we even realise it. It is probably a very good idea to get rid of any alcohol you have in your house right now. There is no need to have temptation right under your nose. Don't go down the alcohol aisle in the supermarket and, in the short term, there is really no need to go into pubs. Don't kid yourself that you can go and have a couple of soft drinks – you may be able to at first, but if you put yourself in the same situations as when you used to drink, you will inevitably find that you will. If there are celebrations or events coming up that you have to attend, where there will be a lot of drinking, arrive late and leave early. Prepare an excuse in advance, so that if you feel unsteady you can leave quickly. Don't worry about offending people. Take responsibility for your sobriety by putting down boundaries that protect you.

Deal with your emotions. These might well be all over the place to begin with and can often feel overwhelming. You may feel angry and resentful, frustrated or full of self-pity, guilt and loneliness, or you may just feel numb. This is to be expected as you have been suffocating and hiding these feelings for a long time. Your feelings may be the reasons you drank or used drugs in the first place. These feelings can't be avoided and need to be felt and processed, but you don't have to do this alone. First of all, recognise what you're feeling and develop different ways of dealing with feelings. It may help to write these feelings down and talk about them to a friend who'll listen, but not judge you. Often, intense negative emotions can be triggered if you feel:

- Hungry
- Angry
- Lonely
- Tired
- Stressed.

Feeling one or more of the above is enough to put you on the edge. Don't underestimate how powerful these emotions are and how quickly they can weaken your defences. Begin recognising how you are feeling.

Loneliness can sometimes creep up on us, especially if we used alcohol to socialise. It's very important that you meet people who don't drink, with whom you can socialise. One of the myths of sobriety is that it's boring and there is nothing to do. This couldn't be further from the truth. Everyone I know who doesn't drink has a jam packed social life, full of exciting things they never would have dreamed of doing before. However, it will take time to build this up, and you need to take responsibility for this. If you have decided to join Alcoholic Anonymous you will find this happens very easily, as AA is a good place to meet lots of sober people! If not, then look at other avenues where you can meet people who don't drink.

Lastly, take it easy! You didn't create your problems overnight and you won't get rid of them overnight either. Accept that you are at the starting point and change will happen slowly, but it will happen. Congratulate yourself that you have decided to take drastic action for your problem and things will get better from this point onwards. There may be some bumps in the road ahead, but you are on the path to recovery now; life will begin to get better, you will begin to feel better about yourself.

Living sober is infinitely easier than struggling with alcoholism.

How to deal with friends who drink

Sometimes when we stop drinking we find we have very few friends left, because we have isolated ourselves from the world. We usually start drinking on our own because we have pushed everyone away; we are filled with shame and remorse over our behaviour and it is easier to shut the world away rather than face people. If this is the case, then life in sobriety can bring new relationships and friendships.

Companionship is vital to human beings and alcoholics seem to have a tendency to isolate. Learning to be part of the human race again is part of the journey in sobriety.

For some people, when they get sober, they still have a social life with friendships intact and some of these friends may drink. Some of these may even drink heavily or alcoholically, but as a newly sober person you are going to have to learn how to deal with them.

Drinking is often a group activity. Groups are very powerful entities. We are generally attracted to groups who reflect back to us who we are, so it is very likely that we drank with people who drank like us. When we stop, it can often upset a group dynamic – you are part of a group all drinking in the same way, but then one of you stops. So what does this say about everyone else? The group may find this hard to deal with; some members may even try to tell you that you're not an alcoholic, or try to persuade you to have a drink.

Just think about that for a second. *How would they know?*

The truth is, if your peer group is trying to persuade you that you don't have a drink problem, it's because they feel uncomfortable about their own drinking. It's easier for them to encourage you to start drinking than to take a look at their *own* drinking. Their drinking is their business and your sobriety is yours. It really comes down to this: true friends will understand, encourage and support you. Your real friends will do things with you that don't involve alcohol. Learn to tell the difference between 'drinking buddies' and true friendship.

It's true that a lot of your friends may not understand why you have decided to stop drinking. Most people have an image of an alcoholic as a 'smelly old man on a bench drinking out of a cheap bottle'. This is a misconception. We have already explored how alcoholism can present itself in many forms. Having a job and a mortgage doesn't make you immune.

Alcoholism is an equal opportunity disease.

There is an interesting stage of readjustment ahead. At first you will want to avoid the big drinking occasions that you would normally attend with your friends. As you go on with your sobriety you may feel more confident to socialise when other people are drinking moderately.

The great news is that you only have to avoid alcohol in the early days; it gets easier and easier and eventually becomes a 'non-issue'. I always compare it to being vegetarian. You just no longer notice the things you don't eat on the menu. Most recovered alcoholics I know, who have long-term sobriety, are undisturbed around alcohol and in drinking environments. They just don't notice it; they are too busy having a good time sober. It doesn't mean that they seek out drinking establishments, rather that if they happen to end up in one to socialise or eat, they can do so with ease and comfort. The fact is that once you get sober, your life tends to expand; you discover there is so much more to do than drink. Life becomes full and interesting in ways you couldn't imagine before.

A love letter to alcohol – saying goodbye

During these first few weeks and months of sobriety you have to face up to saying goodbye to alcohol. It was our best friend, after all. It was always there for us when we needed support or help. This is very much part of the grieving process and can sound strange to someone who hasn't had an alcohol problem. They would surely think we couldn't wait to see the back of it. This isn't always the case. For some of us alcohol was our only friend. It was there when no one else was. Just like a toxic friend or relationship, we have to let it go. Sometimes, after a period of sobriety, we start romanticising our relationship with alcohol. We ignore all the bad stuff and remember only the good: wine with friends, a good brandy, champagne at weddings. It is important to remember our relationship honestly. We simply wouldn't be in this position if our relationship with alcohol had been a good one.

So here is my farewell letter: *Goodbye to alcohol.*

Dear Alcohol,

I don't know where to start. We have come a long way, you and me. Things were great in the beginning. I had never met anyone like you. Nobody had ever made me feel the way you did. I felt special when I was with you. Full of hope, that anything was possible. Those were magical days; no thought of tomorrow, everything ahead of us, exciting and fun. I thought it would always be like that, I thought our feelings would never change. I never believed you could hurt me this much.

You were my world, my everything. You completed me. I felt safe with you. You touched me like no one else could. I came to rely on you. You were always there, wherever I went. Then things changed.

I kept thinking; 'This time it will be different, it will be like the old days'. But it never was, the old days never came back. I tried so hard, but it was all so much simpler in the old days. But you made me feel ashamed. I was scared at what I was capable of when I was with you. I got lost in you. I couldn't see what was really happening. I pushed my family away; my friends didn't matter anymore, as long as I had you.

It stopped being fun a long time ago. I don't remember when. I should have stopped seeing you then, but I couldn't let go of the promise you made all those years ago. You promised you'd be my one and only, but you lied. You lied about everything. I see that now; I see that everything was an illusion, that nothing you did or said was true. How could I have been so stupid, so naive? I was never special to you, you never cared about me. You just wanted me to yourself. You didn't care what I wanted or needed. I was just one more to you. I didn't think there was any further I could go down in my obsession for you, but there was always more pain, more destruction, and still I wouldn't let go. Then I came to the jumping off place. I saw that you would kill me. My love for you would kill me.

I had to learn to live without you.

I decided at that point, that no matter how hard it was I wanted you out of my life forever. You tried to get me back, you were close a couple of times, but finally I saw you as you really were – a liar, a thief, a soul stealer; you were never capable of love. You never cared. It was seeing this that gave me the power to get over you. I learnt that all the things I thought you gave me, I could get myself. I started loving myself; I learnt that I had something to offer. Best of all, I learnt I could cope without you. I found love and connection, in different ways to the ones you offered. What you offered was fake. Now I know what real love is, you could never come close. It's over now, forever. I feel repelled when I see you. I shudder to think that I could ever have loved you, that you could have been important to me. You disgust me. I can walk past you now and it doesn't bother me. I feel free. I feel whole. I can see your lies and laugh at them. You have no hold anymore. You are nothing to me.

Yours sincerely,

A Recovered Alcoholic

Writing this letter helped me enormously. It really was like an obsessive love affair. One I couldn't seem to get over until it took me so far down I knew I was going to die. Facing death is what made me decide to live. I chose life.

The young girl's story

I've included this story here as it is from a girl who was very young when she got sober, eighteen in fact. Hardly enough time to drink and enjoy herself before she was at rock bottom. One of her greatest fears was how dull and boring her life was going to be without alcohol; she didn't think anything would ever be interesting or fun again.

Felicity's story

Ever since I can remember, I have always felt that I wasn't good enough. I always felt I had to prove myself in some way. I was naturally attracted to groups of people who drank or took drugs. When I was fourteen I got involved with a group of people who were significantly older than me. They were aged between eighteen and thirty-five, and I thought my life had begun. I was desperate for them to like me and to be part of their group. So to fit in, I drank and used drugs the way they did. I wanted to belong.

My family fell to pieces quickly as they desperately tried to find out what was wrong with me. My mother was ill from the worry of not knowing where her fourteen year-old daughter might be. I come from a very loving and supportive family and yet I hated to be around them. I felt misunderstood by them. Things got bad very quickly. I lived in squats and became completely dependent on alcohol and drugs and the people around me. I got involved with men who used and abused me for sex. No matter how much my parents tried to help, I just pushed them away. I know now I just didn't know how to accept their love, as I had no love for myself. I abused my body in every way possible and I let others abuse it too. I felt disgusting.

On several occasions I got into trouble with the police because drugs were involved. They set me up with a drugs worker who eventually became a very dear friend to me. She always believed in me and saw past my crap and knew someone special was inside. She knew I loved to sing and act and suggested auditioning for a performing arts school. Having nothing to lose and desperate to do something, I went and they accepted me. At first, I was very happy there, but of course I quickly found the students who drank and took drugs the way I did and my partying took off again.

For my eighteenth birthday my parents paid for my best friend and me to go on holiday. We went to Corfu so we could party. We hit the bars as soon as we arrived and didn't stop. The first couple of weeks were magic, drinking all night and sleeping all day. When the holiday came to an end neither of us wanted to go home. So we didn't.

We stayed and got work doing promotions for a nightclub. This meant I had to dress up every night, flirt and get people to come into the club. But of course it didn't last, soon the amount of alcohol I was consuming made me extremely violent and aggressive. My friends did not want to be around me. I got into regular fights and was extremely abusive and vile.

I was due back at college two days after getting home. I dreaded returning. I felt depressed and drank more than ever. I had also picked up a nasty drug habit while I was away and needed a large amount of booze and cocaine to be able to function. I started to have regular panic attacks and would collapse in class. I was a mess and was the laughing stock of the school.

I lost all my friends and would just lock myself away in my room, which smelt of drink and vomit. I thought about killing myself every day.

At the age of eighteen I finally had a mental breakdown. I was dying and out of desperation I went to my dear friend who'd helped me all those years before and admitted all that had been going on. I told her everything. She arranged for me to go into an addiction treatment centre. I remember feeling a little hope that something was happening; I liked the thought of going to rehab.

There I stood, eighteen years of age, barely the legal age to drink and faced with the fact that I was never going to drink again. I was petrified. I had no idea how to live without alcohol in my life, it just didn't seem possible. It frightened the hell out of me. I began to work really hard on the recovery programme and I started to feel different.

My whole life changed in a few weeks.

It was extremely hard, but I felt incredible. I felt as though chains had been cut. I began to develop amazing relationships with people, being

> a healthy friend, and not letting jealousy, bitterness or resentment stop a relationship from blossoming. People began to love me and accept me for who I was, not what I was pretending to be. I stopped taking everything personally. I stopped blaming everyone else for my problems. Most importantly, I began to build a loving relationship with myself.
>
> *Felicity, 23, sober since 2007*

This story blows me away every time I read it. I wanted to put all of it in this book. I think it is so powerful because Felicity was so young when she hit her rock bottom. Treatment was the intervention she needed to begin to stabilise and understand her problem and a recovery programme gave her what was missing in her life.

I've known Felicity since she was fourteen years old, and never in my wildest dreams did I think that she would change so much so quickly. I believed we would have years of her addiction to live through, with all the wreckage that can cause. She has truly amazed me and I hope she can be an inspiration to other young people, so they can turn their lives around while they are young and not waste more years in the wilderness.

Early recovery is like flying to Barbados

It comes down to what we want our lives to have been about.

Wake up! Your life is happening right now. It's not going to start when you find the right job, house, partner, lose ten pounds. This is not a rehearsal. These precious seconds right now are your life. Are you going to make them count or are you going to fall back into your numbed state and sleepwalk through your life?

I often tell clients that in early recovery, those first few painful months when you 'wake up' to who you are and what you have become are like the experience of when you have to wake up at 3am to catch a flight to Barbados, because you're going on your much anticipated dream holiday.

For those few seconds, when the alarm goes off in the middle of the night, in the pitch black, when you are in the deepest of sleeps, dreaming about a wonderful fantasy, you have to grope around trying to still that intrusive bleeping. Your mind begins an argument with itself, where for a few seconds, you consider just closing your eyes, just for a couple of minutes, to experience that warm, comfortable, seducing lure of sleep again.

Despite *knowing* you don't have long to get to the airport, there is that voice telling you just to shut your eyes and go back to sleep and everything will be OK. The pillow is so soft, the bedding so warm and comfy. The pull is intoxicating. Nothing matters more than the bliss of sleep, of unawareness. But of course you force your tired eyes awake and stand blearily in the shower with the excitement in your belly and the adrenalin beginning to pump through your veins. Because you know that very soon you're going to be on a plane to Barbados and what a wonderful feeling that will be.

The first few months of recovery for an alcoholic are like the first few seconds of being awoken by the alarm clock.

Even though you *know* that where you're going is the most wonderful place you'll ever visit; even though you *know* that this will be the best experience you have ever had and you have been waiting so long for the time to come around; even though you *know* you would be devastated if you gave in and shut your eyes and woke up to realise you'd missed the plane; even though you *know* all of this – there is still a strong temptation to go back to sleep and block out all of those possibilities and experiences for the sake of a few extra hours of nothingness.

This is what the alcoholic experiences in early recovery. For so long they have lived half asleep, half aware, missing their lives, and now finally the opportunity has arrived for them to be fully awake, fully conscious of their experience. But it's very tempting to go back to sleep; this is because recovery is hard and painful at times, especially in the beginning. Even though Barbados will be great, the getting there can sometimes be uncomfortable, painful, irritating and inconvenient. The drive to the airport, carrying bags, queuing at security, airline food, cramped seats, all of those things we would rather do without, but we put up with them because of the *destination.*

The destination for alcoholics is our *truth,* our real, authentic selves, living our lives to the fullest, *being who we really* are – becoming the best version of ourselves we are capable of being.

Have you opened your eyes yet?

Chapter 6

The spiritual aspect of recovery

There is no recovery from alcoholism without spiritual growth. This growth occurs when we let go of, or examine, preconceptions that may block us; when we become open-minded and teachable; when we let the light into our darkness and discover a workable, joyful way of living.

I F SOBRIETY IS really to take hold, it is essential for the alcoholic to develop spiritually. This chapter will explore exactly how spirituality can be defined and how to apply it to our own lives. Spiritual growth must be at the heart of recovery for an alcoholic or they will drink again, or lapse into other unhealthy coping behaviours.

Spirituality can be viewed as a way of having a healthy relationship with yourself, one that is based on self-love, self-esteem and integrity. Addiction can be seen as the opposite of this. Spirituality is about connection. Addiction is defined by disconnection, from self and everything and everyone around you. Spiritual growth is where the richness of life comes from. We are here to grow. Alcoholism prevents this. Spirituality is ultimately the only thing that will fill the 'hole in the soul'. Spirituality is a path that leads us to *wholeness*. It leads us to find self-love, self-esteem and autonomy.

Spirituality can be a tricky subject, and is often met with a lot of prejudice and mis-information. It's important that I clarify what this term means. The mere mention of the word 'spirituality' can send many people screaming from the room. This is because they do a very quick equation in their minds that goes something like this:

Spirituality = God = church = Jesus = nuns = church = boring = pointless = not for me!

This *isn't* what spirituality means. It's an incredibly misunderstood word that can be a very large barrier to people living the life they want. Let me explain. What we have explored so far is that alcoholism and addiction stem from an *internal process*, rather than something that is being *done to us* on the outside. Therefore the solution is internal.

It is an inside job.

You cannot fix an internal problem with an external solution, it has to come from the inside, and that's where spirituality comes in. As we have explored, all behaviour is a manifestation of how we feel. Feelings come from within.

This is the problem, not drink. Drinking has only been an expression of our internal state.

In order to access the internal problem we have to first clear the path, which means you must stop drinking, using drugs or whatever it is you're using to anaesthetise yourself. Alcohol and drugs will always block you from accessing your spirit and fully realising your potential.

What is spirituality?

This is a big question. This chapter is my own and many other people's understanding of the term. Remember, this chapter is about letting go of preconceptions.

Spirituality is not necessarily related to religion. It can be something else altogether, although confusingly it is the basis of *all* religions, if you accept that the explicit purpose of most religions is to take care of our 'souls'.

Our spirit is that voice inside us that is there from the moment we wake up to the moment we go to sleep. It is the conversation we have with ourselves our entire lives.

Our spirit is the *real* us, the part not many other people see.

Our spirit is where our hopes, our dreams, our fears, our secrets, our shame, our joy exist.

It is our intuition, our gut instinct.

It is our sense of right and wrong.

Our spirit is intangible, *but we all know it's there.*

It's what makes you, you. And me, me.

Our spirit is unique to us. *It is us.*

How I feel about other people and the world around me comes from how my spirit responds.

When I fall in love my spirit is ignited. When I am hurt and broken my spirit is crushed.

When I die, for a while you can still touch my body, you can still see me. But I will be gone; my spirit – who I really was – will no longer be there.

You can't touch or hold or control my spirit.

It is me.

That is what our spirits are. Does that make sense? I'll give you an even simpler explanation of spirituality.

Spirituality is just being good to your spirit (your inner-self that no one else sees). *It is honouring who you really are.*

Yep. That's it. How simple is that?

All our pain comes from not looking after our spirit. Not honouring who we really are. When we don't honour it, when we ignore it, when we deliberately crush it, then we slowly begin dying on the inside. This is then reflected in our external world through our behaviour.

Question: does your behaviour honour your spirit – who you really are?

What is the first thing you need to change in order to honour your spirit? I had to stop pouring drink down my throat because it turned me into someone I didn't like. And then I had to stop sleeping with men I didn't like because it made me feel bad about myself (it crushed my spirit). And then I had to stop lying and manipulating. I had to stop binge eating. Then I had to stop people-pleasing and be true to myself. Then I had to stop gossiping because it felt unclean. Then I had to stop chasing money for its own sake, and I had to stop reading glossy women's magazines because I felt shallow.

The list goes on and on and still does. It's a personal list. Nobody can write it for you.

As my spirit awoke, something inside me changed and I found that I couldn't continue with behaviour that harmed me. This didn't change overnight, but it did change at the pace I could handle.

Messes and mistakes

Early on in this spiritual journey I was under the delusion that I had to become perfect at all things and to everyone. After trying this for a while I found I could barely breathe, I was so terrified of making a mistake or messing up! It was then that I realised that the best kind of personal growth came from when I *did* mess up or make a mistake. Having the opportunity to look at my human vulnerability, and how faulty thinking led to bad decisions and their consequences, is what freed me. For the first time in my life I was free to learn, grow and change. And so it has continued, I have never stopped making messes and mistakes; the difference now is that I'm making different ones because I've learnt from the old ones!

I'm finally facing the right direction now and doing the best I can. I am re-connected with my spirit. When I listen to that voice and honour it, I make much better decisions and ultimately take better actions. When I'm connected to *who I really am* it's harder for me to make decisions that are destructive or harmful to myself or others. Destruction and harm are always caused when decisions are made from fear and not truth. It's always clear to me from the consequences of my actions whether I'm 'tuned in' or not.

I realised through my mistakes that most things I used to do no longer remained attractive to me; they were a distraction from my truthful self. When they came to my attention I began to see them for what they were and they held no worth for me. I began to choose things that enriched my spirit rather than crushed it. I began to attract people into my life who could teach me and help me, who are my peers and equals. My fear of other people and what they thought of me began to change through this experience. My inside world had changed so much, that my outside world followed. It was focusing on spiritual growth that enabled the changes I had longed for to actually happen in my life.

How does this come about?

The gift of desperation

It sounds like a really lousy gift, doesn't it? But for many of us it is only when we are at our most desperate that we then take the plunge and look for something more meaningful in our lives, that we look for change. Because alcoholics have known great pain, they are also capable of knowing great joy.

It was only when I reached the point of desperation that I decided I wasn't going to kill myself. I did want to live. *I just didn't know how.* However, I made the decision to do whatever it took to heal my life. At first I was only interested in some peace of mind. I couldn't continue to live with the storm in my head. I knew I had to put down the drink and drugs.

I didn't believe happiness was possible for someone like me. I was prepared to settle for some peace. Thankfully, not only was happiness possible in my life, it is now abundant. However, I don't believe I would ever have found my authentic self *without* the gift of desperation. It was desperation that motivated me.

My story

I had always felt so wrong inside, so empty and broken, that these feelings were normal for me; I had nothing to compare them with. I had never experienced real contentment or peace. I didn't know what it was like to like myself, let alone to love myself.

And yet, when I began this journey of spiritual awakening and I took responsibility to peel off the layers that kept me trapped, something incredible happened. It was very subtle. I almost didn't notice that anything had changed, but one day I realised I no longer felt 'wrong'. The feelings of 'wrongness' had just gone, evaporated. After that I understood that it was ridiculous to believe that I was revolting or disgusting; I realised I was just an ordinary human being. I was OK. I no longer hated myself.

Something felt very different inside. I felt lighter, freer, unburdened. I just did the work and the results followed. I liked the results, so I kept doing the work and I've never stopped, because every day I seem to grow a little more, and finally I realised I loved myself.

How was this possible, I thought? For thirty years I had felt so totally wrong, and then in the space of a few months my thinking and belief systems had undergone profound and radical change.

What the gift of desperation taught me is that my former life was the hard one. It wasn't the easier choice, it just seemed that way, but actually the truth was that living as an active alcoholic was very hard work. Constant lies, managing the fear, covering up my drinking, trying to explain the consequences and just messing up, over and over. It was exhausting.

Incredibly, the life I had been avoiding was actually the easier path. Discovering my authentic self, striving to live life authentically and living my truth were so much easier and infinitely more rewarding. Spirituality is ultimately about freedom.

So if you are desperate right now, desperate to change your life, desperate to have some peace, then the good news is, you can. You can start right here by just making a commitment to yourself to do whatever it takes. It will take a lot less than you think. The first step is to put down the drink, get help and consider the fact that you are a spiritual being.

Collete's story

I always envied people who drank with calmness. When I was twelve, I went to a sleepover where we secretly, after midnight, raided the grown-ups' drinks cabinet. I drank half a bottle of whisky and blacked out. I'd never drunk anything before. I woke up the next morning in my friend's mum's newly redecorated attic, to discover I had vomited – quite spectacularly – all over the beige wallpaper, beige carpet and beige futon. I didn't get any pocket money for a year, to repay them.

I write this as a funny anecdote. Because it is funny. It's only when I think about the many times that situation was re-played, in different versions, over the next ten years of my life that it stops being funny and makes me sad. Sad and tired. I won't list what I drank or popped or snorted, I'll just say that I spent my formative years barely clinging onto the edges, always hung-over, always either scowling or wailing with laughter.

I woke up in a hotel room with a strange man asking for my credit card. I was carried out of a nightclub, frothing at the mouth. I was rushed off to hospital twice and put in the resuscitation unit. My arms went blue due to vasoconstriction from the drugs I was taking. Writing this down, the stories sound almost sensationalist. But it's not a Tarantino movie – there was no glamour. At the same time, I did well at school. I went to university. I excelled and was congratulated for all kinds of things. So I convinced myself that this was the life I was supposed to live.

I became used to the fact that my own head was a dark place to be. My silent mantra was, 'If you leave me alone, I will be unkind to myself'. Sometimes I'd take a secret, bitter pride in this. Other times I'd want someone else to take away the pain for me – and I expected this from my romantic partners. It never occurred to me that the remedy could be inside; that my heart could have its own cleansing properties. For a long time, I thought being sad was the normal neutral emotion for everybody. I thought waking up in the morning and feeling sad was the normal start to the day, and something great would have to happen in order to make me feel happy. I didn't know how to feel good about myself just by sitting in a chair, or walking down the street. I was depressed, but I didn't have the self-esteem to realise that I deserved a better inner world.

When I was twenty-two, things became unmanageable. I was lucky, really, to hit rock bottom so hard, so young – because there was no denying it. My family and friends were all terrified. I had stopped caring. I had gone past drinking without calmness, and started drinking and using with intent. I didn't want to die but I couldn't cope with being alive. This is why I am immensely grateful to have had the support, finances and opportunity to be packaged off to rehab, because my willpower was non-existent. I needed to be plonked in an institution in the middle of the desert with no way of getting my hands on anything. And that is literally what happened. Once the booze and chemicals were out of my system, however, I was a willing guest in that place. I was broken and ashamed, but relieved. I wanted to get better and I ended up staying in treatment for six months, attending meetings every day.

After a year of tiptoeing around, I finally became voluntarily single for the first time in six years. Now I live alone in my flat. All my friends in rehab told me living alone was a bad idea – 'don't trust yourself' – but I realised that in order for my recovery to be worth something, I needed to step out into the sky and trust I would land on my feet. I needed to enjoy my own company. Now my career is going well, I feel like a responsible adult for the first time, and my family and friends don't worry about me any more than I worry about them. And that feels a lot like freedom.

Collette, 25, sober since 2009

The authentic self

When we looked at the problem of alcoholism we saw how the alcoholic gradually loses themselves. By that, I mean they lose their sense of self, they become disconnected from who they really are. We also saw how alcohol numbs the unbearable pain of this. Recovery is about reconnection to that sense of self.

This is spiritual work.

Becoming authentic does not mean becoming perfect. That is a faulty belief and very limiting. It just means *facing the right way.* Being on the path to authenticity, rather than lost in the woods. It is a journey.

To live authentically is to begin the journey of knowing yourself. Finding out what is really inside, what you have been covering up all these years.

"Most people will be able to relate to the notion of a dimension which represents their ideas and beliefs about life, the world, themselves and the beyond. The spiritual world is the domain of experience where people create meaning for themselves and make sense of things."
Van Deurzen, 2002

Inner world evaluation

We can live a lifetime without knowing who we really are. That is a tragedy. This is particularly true of alcoholics. The purpose of this exercise is to begin to dig deeper, to start the discovery process. It is designed to get you asking profound questions of yourself. There are no right or wrong answers. A very good principle my counselling tutor taught me was to '*observe yourself with curiosity, not judgement*'. This is what I would like to invite you to begin to do.

All the answers to the following questions will come from within. You will know the answers. You always have, you just didn't listen. Now is the time to practise real self-honesty, to *listen* to that voice inside you, and to *trust* what it says.

1) What lights up my soul and brings me joy? It doesn't matter how small or insignificant, just list everything or everyone that makes your soul light up (eg some particular music, a certain place or person).

2) What are my secret fears? Again, it doesn't matter how small or insignificant, just begin to identify and list all the things you have kept hidden that frighten you (eg rejection, the dark…).

3) Who would I be if I were free from these fears? Just try to imagine what kind of person you would be if you didn't have these fears, if they were removed. What would you do?

4) What is the best thing about me? Don't say 'nothing'! Most people find it hard to say anything positive about themselves. Alcoholics are no different. But there *is* something: maybe you have a great laugh, or are kind to strangers. Don't be shy. Think back and identify the parts of yourself you do like.

5) In my last days, as I look back over my life, what do I want it to have been about? This is a very powerful question, so take time to think it over, no matter how old you are or what your life is like at this precise moment. The future is ahead of you. It has yet to be determined. You have time to remake it into what you want. So imagine now what you want that to be about.

These are *powerful* questions and you may feel you don't know the answers to them, or the answers you do get may even frighten you. Please don't panic. You don't have to change your whole life in the next 24 hours. All you have to do is awaken and understand that this is a journey that will take the rest of your life and can start today.

It starts with *knowing*, really knowing yourself. By starting this process you are also on the path to self-acceptance. We are not looking for perfection here. What we are doing is trying to be the best version of ourselves we are capable of being. That means accepting our human-ness, embracing our imperfections, and accepting that we are just works in progress. You are neither good nor bad. As alcoholics, we may in the past have behaved badly, but that does not mean we, ourselves, are bad. As we move forward, we have to take responsibility for our behaviour, good and bad, whether it was under the influence of alcoholism or not. We also have to forgive ourselves and begin learning from the way we feel and how we behave. This is growth. Spiritual growth.

Letting go of spiritual beliefs imposed upon you

The reason that we find it so hard sometimes to embrace spiritual con-cepts is that we are prejudiced by limiting beliefs. The words 'spiritual-ity', and 'God' specifically, are very loaded for most people. Sometimes the meanings we have attached to these words prevent us from being open to other interpretations. Often, the reason for this is that we have picked up our beliefs and prejudices along the way. This has prevented us from developing our own beliefs.

All I'm asking you to do is to examine your beliefs and where they come from. These beliefs can be ingrained in us and are very hard to let go of. I'm not asking you to do anything drastic. Just to recognise that you are responsible for your own spiritual growth. This may mean leav-ing behind lifelong prejudices. It certainly means keeping an open mind, and having a willingness to explore concepts before passing judgments. Most of all, it means recognising that you are a spiritual being.

Letting go of religion and finding God

I'm including this story to demonstrate how powerful our preconceived ideas and beliefs are, how damaging they can be. I watched Andy go through agony wrestling with his childhood conceptions of 'God'. It was destroying him and he found it impossible to let go. Eventually he had to and he now sees 'God' as essential to his recovery and happiness. The difference is that he defined for himself what the word 'God' meant. No one else did it for him. He now loves himself and is not full of guilt and shame. He is free.

Andy's story

Finding a concept of God that worked for me seemed very sensible and straightforward when it was suggested to me when I stopped drinking, although I thought it was somewhat unnecessary. Because I had been quite active in church I assumed it would not be a problem, 'This will be easy,' I thought to myself. Despite not having had a religious upbringing in my family of origin, and having been a very naughty boy, I had always gravitated towards religion. Thus, I supposed, it would be only a matter of slightly adjusting my old belief system to my current circumstances.

This is a journey that started when I was twenty years old. At this point I had no idea of the profound implications of having to find a relationship with God as I understood him. It never occurred to me that every time I left church after attending Mass and confessing my sins to the priest, the horrible guilt and fear I felt when I did something 'wrong' were connected to a deep feeling of being bad, someone who deserved to be punished.

I would seek confession with different priests to avoid being caught out. I knew there was something wrong but did not know exactly what it was, let alone how to solve it. I started looking for help in different 12-step fellowships and in self-help books. Anything I could get my hands on would be devoured quickly, looking for the silver bullet. I got tired and decided that the sin concept was what really caused the harm, so I decided to stop attending church and gave in to compulsive sex, relationships and food. Those did not work either, and after a few years I felt suicidal and desperate. Later on I looked for help to solve the new problems I had created.

The work I had to do to stop the above set off my real growth. I managed to stop the self-destructive behaviours more or less successfully, at least at the physical level. However, anger, resentment and fear came up to the surface. The first time someone suggested I was resentful towards God I got terrified. If that was true it was definitely unacceptable; how could someone hate God and get away with it? At this point I was far from thinking I had to change my concept of God and how I viewed myself. However, my anger increased until I was suicidal again, then I reached the point at which I was willing to do whatever I could to relieve this pain. That is when I was ready to let go of my religion and its concept of God.

Since my prayers to the God of my religion were not working anymore, in the midst of a great emotional struggle I decided to pray to the Spirit of the Universe. I prayed to that Supreme Being who created the sky, the oceans, and my brothers and sisters from other species. It was a neutral concept, which departed from all the religious connotations that prevented me from getting to know a loving God. On the one hand, I was scared of having made a decision that later on I would regret whilst facing death. 'What if all these Catholics were right after all and I will end up in hell?' I thought to myself. On the other hand something told me I had made the right decision, that I was not betraying Jesus.

As I continued my process of self-discovery and change, I realised that although it was not the entire fault of the religion in which I was raised, the concept of God it promoted no longer worked for me. I could not get my head around the idea of God punishing me if I do not stick to the Ten Commandments. What kind of love is that? The only way to stop hating God would be by letting go of my old beliefs and getting new ones. I decided that from that point on, my God was going to be loving, forgiving, compassionate, powerful, and that no matter what I did, punishment did not exist for him. So I came to this: when I suffer as a consequence of self-imposed crises, he also suffers, and is right there with me. He also respects my freedom and wants me to be strong, that is why he lets me make choices – regardless of how destructive they might be – and does not do for me what I can do for myself.

Even my perception of religion has changed. Now I know that traditional, organised religion is not the best way for me to connect with God, and that like any other human affairs, it is right about a lot of things but is also full of mistakes. Furthermore, I know that not everything religion promotes is necessarily God's will, and that there are many ways in which people from all walks of life can connect with him. That is how I finally came to re-encounter my loving, compassionate and powerful Father, who never left me, was there for me, suffered alongside me when I did, and who always wants the best for me.

Andy, 40, sober since 1992

Removing obstacles

Some people feel resistant to getting help for alcohol problems because they feel they can't relate to spiritual concepts. They hear the word 'spirituality' or 'God' and they balk. Some of the reasons people feel resistance to spiritual concepts are:
- They are atheist, and believe there is no God.
- They are agnostic, and believe there is no proof of a God.
- They have had an unpleasant or abusive experience at the hand of a member of a church or religious organisation.
- The perceived hypocrisy of religious people.
- They recognise the role of religion in wars and conflict and do not wish to be associated with it.
- They believe religion is about being controlled.
- They are uncomfortable with religious teachings like the concept of sin and resurrection.
- Witnessing abuse and suffering in the world, they do not understand why God does nothing about it.
- Fear of ridicule about spiritual beliefs.
- Unpleasant experiences as a child with organised religion.
- Fear of not living up to the expectations of the religion they were raised in.

This is just a sample of what some clients express to me when I begin to introduce spiritual concepts to them. These are all understandable reasons for questioning the validity of spirituality and the concept of God, but they should not stop you from discovering your own spiritual path. The impact of organised religion cannot be underestimated, both good and bad, but it is entirely up to you what you keep and what you reject. Your path may be to stay within your religion – this may be your spiritual truth – or you may take a different path. Only you can make that decision.

Connecting with your spiritual self

Wholeness is our goal: to be whole, fully functioning human beings. Connecting with ourselves, our internal self, our spiritual self, is as easy or as difficult as we want to make it. We just need to start. Instead of a lifetime of running away, we are going to be still, be in the moment, connected to who we really are.

You are not required to become a spiritual guru, to wear sandals and meditate for hours a day. You can if you wish, you just don't *have* to in order to walk a spiritual path. It's your path, you get to choose the shoes you walk in.

I would start by learning more about spiritual concepts. Get a book or DVD. Go and talk to someone who seems to be interested in spirituality. Do some investigating. All you need in early recovery is to be open-minded to how important spiritual growth is to recovery from alcoholism.

This is just a start. This chapter was about getting you thinking about spiritual concepts in a way that's right for you. The next chapter will explore in depth the different factors that block our spiritual growth, and how to overcome them.

Chapter 7

Overcoming the blocks to recovery

Managing your emotional life is crucial to maintaining sobriety. This means dealing with both the positive and negative aspects of your feelings. Understanding our emotional lives is vital for balance and happiness.

Restoring balance

I F ALL YOU needed to do to stop drinking was to stop drinking, then everyone with a drinking problem would have stopped drinking and everything would be fine. But it's never as simple as that, is it? There's so much more to stopping drinking than putting down the drink.

This chapter will provide an overview of the key parts of an alcoholic personality. It will explore how these traits drive alcoholism and how they can be overcome. In many ways these personality traits are no different from anyone else's – they cause pain and discomfort – except that with an alcoholic, if they are not overcome, they will inevitably lead to destructive drinking.

This is because pride, shame, guilt and fear all block us from spiritual growth and we have already established how essential this is for sobriety. Shame, guilt, belief systems, pride and so on, are all interlinked and in many ways can't be dealt with separately. I want to provide an insight into all these areas so the alcoholic can identify which ones affect them the most and begin to form strategies to deal with them.

Understanding and dealing with your emotions

There is just no getting away from it. We have to deal with this emotional pain that has fuelled our alcoholism and other unhealthy behaviours. The goal here is mastery over our emotions. Our feelings and emotions can often be overwhelming, making us feel like little boats being tossed about on a huge ocean.

This is not a problem exclusive to alcoholics. The themes explored in this chapter relate to many people, not just drinkers. But while non-drinkers may have the luxury of not learning about and managing their emotions, alcoholics do not. Our methods of dealing with emotional pain are so severe, and affect so many people, that we cannot ignore dealing with them.

Emotions are really nothing more than currents of energy that flow through us in order to relay information about how our thinking is working. It is how we process this information that is key.

Each emotion we feel contains a message that we have to process. It is a message from our soul. If we ignore the message, by drinking or trying to change outside circumstances in order to change our emotions, then the message will just return. It will keep on returning until we listen to the message.

Our emotions are there to provide us with vital information. If we ignore them then we ignore the information and we stay stuck. Emotions and feelings are actually our friends. They are there to serve us, not to work against us. So the first step is to listen to our emotions and to begin to understand what they are saying to us.

In many ways there are only two basic emotions: fear and love; all other emotions stem from them. Anger, jealousy, greed, spite and vengeance are just different forms of fear. Joy, gratitude and happiness are forms of love. Different events and circumstances will elicit different emotions from us. It is our job to recognise these emotions when they present and seek the message inside them.

All human beings have basic needs. We have physical needs for shelter, warmth, food and so on. We also have spiritual needs. We need to feel safe, valued and loved. Often, when we have strong negative emotions it's because these basic needs are threatened.

Take anger, for instance. Anger is a very powerful emotion, and we may find ourselves getting angry in circumstances we don't fully understand. We may think we are angry because someone has made us angry, but in reality we are angry because one of our spiritual needs has been threatened. Or rather, we *perceive* it to be threatened. So we are not really angry, we are frightened that we are not going to be loved, or that our safety is threatened or that we are not being valued. When we begin to understand this, the task of unravelling our emotions becomes easier.

We can then begin to understand why we are angry or frightened and take the necessary steps to fix the situation. These steps are internal. We will not solve this problem by rearranging our external circumstances.

In this way, we can start thinking of our emotions and feelings as an internal navigation system – specifically designed to get us where we want to go.

Internal navigation systems and how to use them

Imagine the following scenario: you are a pilot who intends to fly to Russia, but as you are taking off you decide you know how to get there, so you ignore all of your instruments (which are designed to show you where to go) and just fly in the direction you think Russia to be. Because you were so sure you knew where to go and that your knowledge would get you there, you would probably be very surprised if you landed in the North Pole. You would be confused and embarrassed to have ended up in a completely different place to the one you thought you were going to.

Well, a pilot flying a plane without using their navigation system is like a person trying to live a successful life without utilising their emotions to guide them effectively. They think they are heading towards the destination of happiness and contentment but end up instead in the country of despair and frustration. There is a big difference between being ruled by your emotions and utilising their messages effectively.

Our internal navigation system is a vital tool that we use in order to get where we need to go. Feelings are there to serve us, not the other way round. Our feelings simply indicate what our *truth* is and the direction we need to take.

Most people take action based on what they think or what they want, ignoring the signals their feelings are sending them. Fear drives us to take actions that our inner voice is screaming its protest against, and yet we ignore it. We are acting on fear rather than truth. I remember so many times saying 'yes' to something I didn't want to do because I was afraid of disappointing the person asking me. I was frightened of being rejected, so I went against the voice inside me and would inevitably end up in a worse predicament because I hadn't listened to the messages my feelings were trying to send me.

Sometimes we feel bad after we have taken an action and we later realise we have made the wrong choice *because our feelings have told us so.* This is a normal part of being human. When a similar situation occurs again our feelings send us messages 'Remember this, remember what we don't want to happen here?'. And bingo, we make a different choice with different consequences. We make mistakes and that's how we learn. *However,* some of us repeat the same mistakes over and over again, because we don't listen to our feelings.

Our feelings are there to help us understand and navigate *before* we act. Everyone has had the experience of their gut instinct saying one thing but their thoughts saying another, and then acting *against* their feelings and regretting it. When there is a 'separation of self', the mind and our feelings (our truth) are often working against each other. Our minds are often in a place of fear, so they will be telling us one thing whilst our feelings may be telling us another. Our minds can carry a lot of rubbish around in them, often stuff we have picked up from other people, unhelpful rules, limiting beliefs and so on. We can also get caught up in other's opinions of what we should do. Our goal is for our minds and hearts to work in unity, because they both contain essential information for our wellbeing.

To use our internal navigations systems more effectively we have to learn how to listen to what our emotions are telling us *'Is this a good idea for me? Maybe I should say no? This opportunity feels right.',* and so on.

We are all naturally intuitive beings, some of us have just forgotten how to use the skill. Next time you have to make a decision or choice, listen to the feelings running through your body. What are they trying to say? You will make mistakes and think you have a gut instinct when you don't. That is all good learning practice. This is a skill that takes practice and you can get better at over time.

Dealing with the past

We all have a past. We all have a past that contains things we would rather not remember. Alcoholics, especially, can have quite messy pasts. Sometimes these pasts haunt our present, and it is for this reason that we need to face them at some point. In early recovery (the first months) I would strongly suggest that you leave the past to one side while you focus on maintaining your sobriety and becoming emotionally stronger. There will be time later to get 'closure' on past events. None of us can change the past, but we can change how we feel about it. That is what closure is. Many alcoholics and addicts have experienced horrific abuse in the past and this has gone on to shape much of their lives. Abuse, particularly if it was sexual, can seem very difficult to get over. It can, for many years, be the reason someone drank, to block out the pain. At some point this abuse needs to be processed and dealt with. Healing can and needs to take place. It's possible to overcome the most horrific past and to lead a healthy, happy, fulfilling life. I've seen it many times with numerous clients, whose courage and tenacity have left me speechless.

Let me be clear. The past, no matter how bad it was, can be overcome. However, it needs to happen when you're ready. We can come to terms with everything that happened to us and everything we did that may have made us ashamed or embarrassed. There are a very few alcoholics who have not behaved in some way that they later find humiliating and shameful. You are not alone.

I can remember countless incidents from the past when I said or did things that I would later regret and feel terrible about. It was just another way to beat myself up. It confirmed what a terrible human being I really was.

I told lies, cheated, was fickle, stole, manipulated and I was false, nasty, dishonest and horrible. I am all of these things and worse when I am engaged in active alcoholism. What I mean by this is that I didn't just behave badly when I was drunk (which I did, often) I could equally behave badly when not drinking. My behaviour changed completely when I got sober permanently and developed my spiritual life. Through this I became a whole person. When you are whole it is much harder to behave in such terrible and selfish ways.

Over time, with work and by taking responsibility for myself, I began to be free of my past. I forgave myself, learnt the lessons and let go. Now, I don't feel ashamed and embarrassed when I remember different incidents, instead I know they were the behaviours of a very damaged, very frightened person, who just didn't know any better at the time.

In time, you will forgive yourself too. You will also overcome your past. If you are not ready to look at past traumas, that's OK. Focus on your sobriety, get stronger, and in time you will be free too.

Shame and guilt

Shame and guilt are common blocks. We pick these up very young and carry them around with us for our entire lives without realising this was completely unnecessary, and that the shame and guilt didn't belong to us in the first place. They weigh us down.

We feel guilty when we have done something to make us feel ashamed; it's usually when we do something that is against our own morals or values, or something that makes another person feel bad.

Shame is the feeling we get when we do something that disappoints someone else. We have a strong feeling of shame when we believe we aren't good enough; we become ashamed of who we are.

The difference between guilt and shame is this, we feel guilt when we behave badly; we feel shame because we believe we *are* bad.

Most of us carry shame and guilt without even knowing it. We can also pick up a lot of shame and guilt that doesn't even belong to us, particularly from family members. In order to be free from shame we need to deal with its root causes. We feel ashamed for a variety of reasons. We can pick up a feeling of shame in childhood that stems from unhealthy limiting beliefs that we are not good enough. We will also feel ashamed if we have been abused in some way. Abused people pick up the shame that actually belongs to the abuser and they carry it around, sometimes for a lifetime.

Recognise this. Recognise that any shame you feel because of what was done to you *is not yours.* You can put it down.

We also feel ashamed when we are doing something that doesn't fit with our image of ourselves. Perhaps we were promiscuous, or lied about money, or stole. In order not to feel ashamed any more, we have to address the behaviour and change that.

I often find that when clients feel guilty, this feeling is often 'given' to them by a parent or older sibling. Parents have an amazing ability to make us feel guilty about what we're doing. This isn't usually intentional, but it is often used as a form of manipulation. In turn, we also make other people feel guilty in order to get what we want. How many times have you *known* you were making your friend or partner feel guilty in order to get your own way?

Guilt is a form of control. We use it to get what we want. If you are a chronic people pleaser then you are going to be very susceptible to manipulation by others because you will feel guilty if you don't please them.

Here's the news. You are responsible for how you feel. So recognise the *transaction of guilt* between people. Recognise when you use it and when others use it on you. Stop using it on others. It is not an honest way of communicating. It may bring you short-term results, but at the cost of your integrity. Recognise when others use it on you and refuse to buy into it. Don't pick up what is not yours. If you suspect someone will feel bad because of what they have done, don't try to rescue them; if you do you will you rob them of a learning experience from which they may grow.

Imagine guilt as a heavy box on the floor that someone implicitly asks you to carry. How will you feel if you pick it up? Will you be able to manoeuver through the rest of your day carrying the box, or will it make life difficult and awkward? Would you be able to do all of things you would like to do? Of course not!

Leave the box where it is. It isn't yours. Imagine how free you would be if you no longer had to carry it. Excuse yourself from the grown up game of pass the parcel. Life will be a lot lighter if you do.

Andrew's story

I drank on a daily basis for thirty-five years. And it was always one foot on the brake and one on the accelerator. I never drank normally. During my neurotic relationship with alcohol I lost my judgement, my ability to express my feelings and conduct relationships of trust and, towards the end of my drinking, was losing my health, mind and spirit. What was left? Not much that I wanted. I was a liar, a thief and a manipulator who was only looking out for himself, trying to maintain my drinking and stay sane, and all the while denying I had a problem.

By the time I put up my hand and asked for help, alcohol had taken over my life. I simply could not stand myself any longer, and the daily grind of waking ill, swearing off booze and then drinking again, *against my will*, wore me down. I couldn't stand myself. I knew I had to deal with my drinking or go under.

I have not had a drink for many years now. I went into rehab and joined AA – two of the most significant moves I have ever made. My gratitude is very, very real. I celebrate this gratitude every day, in all aspects of my life. Every morning now I wake clear headed and relish the possibilities. I can, and do, express my feelings. My relationships are cleaner, straighter. I laugh a lot. I am a pleasure to be around. *I like myself.*

My life in general is full of hope, interest, love and joy. I have entered that bright, clean room I used to dream about. And do I miss alcohol? I do not. This, for me, is the miracle. This obsession has been taken away from me. I can now take life as it is, unvarnished, no blockers needed. I can now *live*.

Andrew, 57, sober since 2006

Pride

Pride, and the lies we tell ourselves, kills more alcoholics than anything else. Living this way is like living in a self-imposed prison. We are never free of what we *think* other people think about us.

Pride is fear-based: fear of what we *think* other people think of us, or caring too much about the opinion of others. The more we fuel this type of thinking the more powerful and impenetrable our pride becomes. When we are prideful we will do whatever we can to prevent people seeing the real us. This is why pride can kill. It can be so powerful it actually prevents people asking for the help they desperately need, because they are scared of what someone else will think!

When we take actions based on pride they will inevitably be the wrong ones because they are not based on our own personal integrity. We are not using our navigation system to guide us.

The thing about pride is that it all takes place in our own imagination, which frankly is not always to be trusted. Think about it: *pride is about what you think others think of you.* You don't even know it for sure! It's only what you suspect or imagine. In reality you are creating these thoughts from faulty beliefs: fear and self-delusion – they are not real and anyway: *what other people think about you is none of your business*!

That's right. Shocked? Well it's the truth. Your thoughts are your own thoughts. They are private to you. And my thoughts are my thoughts, private to me.

Our thoughts are organic and change and fluctuate all the time. Often what we think one day is ridiculous to us the next. Well, this is the same for other people.

Could you be free now? Imagine this: being free of what others may or may not think of you, free to act regardless of what others think. A little suggestion here: this only works when we act in accordance with our internal navigation system. If you endeavour to act with truth and integrity, striving to be free of guilt and pride, your internal navigation system will work effectively and you will be free to be who you are. Again, this is not about being perfect, it's just trying to be better than we were.

Anger

Anger is a complicated and frightening emotion. I've heard it described as 'fear announced'. There is a lot of truth in this. Often, we get angry because we are actually frightened. We feel threatened in some way and respond with anger. Anger is not an emotion we want to get rid of entirely, it can be a useful emotion when used well. But if we fail to understand it, then it can be a dangerous and destructive force in our lives. Anger is what drives us to change. When we see injustice, intolerance, hate or prejudice to individuals or groups, it is anger at these situations that motivates us to do something about them. So an angry response is sometimes appropriate. What we don't want, is to be ruled by anger. Anger works against us when we *act with anger* inappropriately to events that happen to us. For example, if someone cuts us up when we are driving, we may feel annoyed for a few seconds, but prolonged anger about this for the rest of the day is inappropriate and unhealthy. Anger can exhibit itself in many ways.

Here are some of the ways it manifests:

- Violence – either to self, others or objects.
- Withholding – physically and emotionally withdrawing from the person you are angry at; ignoring them and refusing to reveal what is wrong.
- Bullying – name calling, confrontational behaviour, aggression.
- Passive aggression – being a 'martyr', behaving in a certain way because you know it will upset someone; withholding attention; all forms of manipulation.
- Hostility – hostile people are angry at everyone; they have an invisible wall around them that says 'Do Not Enter'.
- Sarcasm – making frequent flippant comments or cutting remarks disguised as humour; using facial expressions or tone of voice to express disapproval.

All of these are different ways in which anger is expressed. You may recognise yourself or other people in these descriptions.

The first stage in getting your anger under control is to recognise your anger and then begin to identify the different triggers. Sometimes, when we allow ourselves to get angry, it's because we have put unrealistic expectations on ourselves and then get angry with ourselves for not achieving them, or at others because we have perceived that they have prevented us from achieving them.

A mother is angry with her four year-old because they are always late for nursery. A boss is always angry with himself for never achieving everything he set out to do that day. A woman is angry at the traffic jam because she is going to miss her meeting.

Sometimes we are just angry at the world because it isn't doing what we want it to do, and we feel we have to blame someone.

Looking at our expectations can sometimes be a way to reduce some of our anger, especially that directed at other people. No one is ever going to do what you want in the way you want it done, especially traffic, four year-olds, employees or family members. Now, we can continue to feel frustrated and angry at things or people not doing what we want, or we can begin to accept things as they are and change our response. If I've left enough time for my journey and am unexpectedly delayed in traffic, there is nothing I can do about that situation. I did my best. I can call ahead and let people know I am delayed, and I can sit back and wait. These events are beyond my control.

This isn't going to be fixed overnight, but we can make small advances by just recognising when and how we get angry and asking ourselves if there is perhaps a better response, especially to events that are simply beyond our control. In early recovery, it's especially important to recognise our anger triggers and choose different responses. Anger can very often lead to picking up a drink, because we believe drink is the only thing that will 'calm us down'. It doesn't. Mix alcohol with anger and what you often get is anger turning inward and becoming self-pity and depression. Or it becomes explosive, like a Molotov cocktail, and results in violence of some kind. The anger is looking for some kind of release, some way to express itself. Alcohol provides a release – a destructive and ineffective one (no growth or learning occurs), but a release nonetheless.

Instead, when you feel yourself becoming angry, ask yourself this, 'What am I frightened of?'. This may lead to a more honest answer or response. If someone is angry at their four year-old for messing around in the mornings, the mother may actually be frightened that she isn't a good mother because her child isn't obedient.

So, in these early stages, be aware of what makes you angry. Identify different possible responses when you can. Recognise the fear that is lurking underneath. Over time you can take further steps to get your anger under control.

Fear

We have already looked at how fear can dominate the life of an alcoholic and how fear is at the root of alcoholism. Ironically, one of the biggest fears an alcoholic can have is giving up alcohol, because they are so frightened of how they will cope without it. I want to assure you that you can cope with your fear sober.

In fact, it will be easier to cope with your fears now you are not drinking. Over time, you will be able to deal with all of your fears appropriately, and drinking to cope with them will be the last thing on your mind. Like anger, we don't want to get rid of fear completely, it is a necessary emotion that is there to serve, if used correctly.

Fear is what motivates us to teach our children to cross the road properly and to learn to swim. Fear (and anger) is what motivates us to protest against wars and nuclear armament. Fear can motivate us to take health precautions when necessary. So it has its uses, in small doses and directed appropriately. The trouble is, alcoholics have let fear get so out of control that it dominates their lives.

Getting sober also means not running away from our fears any longer. Instead, we are going to deal with them more effectively. This is also a process that will continue throughout early recovery. Fear is part of growth. We have to grow as human beings, so we have to learn how to deal with it.

I think that in very early recovery (the first three months), alcoholics can be frightened about a lot of things related to their drinking:

- Do other people realise I had an alcohol problem?
- Have I damaged my body?
- Does my boss realise I had an alcohol problem?
- How will I cope without alcohol?
- How will I deal with social situations?
- What do other people think of me?
- Will my spouse/partner leave me?
- Have I ruined my life?

You will notice that all of these questions can invoke fear if you let them. In the early days it is important to begin to look at things differently. It's easy to let your thoughts get out of control when thinking something like 'Does my boss know I had an alcohol problem?'. If left unchecked you could start thinking, 'Maybe they'll use this to get rid of me. Maybe they are planning to fire me. How will I cope without my job? How will I pay the mortgage? We'll lose the house. My partner will leave me if I don't have a job. How will I ever be able to face anyone? I'll be a laughing stock.'.

See how that thinking increases your fear?

Instead, let's be a bit more realistic. Maybe your boss does know, but you have been good at your job in the past, so they are willing to give you a chance if you get sober. Even if they want to fire you, you may be protected by law; clarify this by speaking to a lawyer or to your Human Resources department. Despite what you feel, you will find that friends, families and co-workers may actually be admiring and supportive of your decision to get sober. People will respect you for holding your hand up, admitting you have a problem and doing something about it.

Take a risk, with someone you can trust who is generally supportive of you; admit honestly what has been happening and what you are doing to help yourself. You will very likely be amazed at their reaction. Generally, when we frankly admit our problems and seek help, other people are enormously supportive of this. If you do something like this it will reduce your fear significantly, as you will be able to see that other people feel similarly. Taking action in this way will enable you to see things differently and therefore to feel differently. Just taking this one action will help you reduce your fear of what other people think, as you will know for certain, rather than just guessing. And you will lose the fear of consequences, because people are usually very reasonable when you are frank and honest with them. If, however, you find someone has a negative reaction, try not to take it badly. People directly affected by your drinking will naturally harbour feelings of resentment and bitterness. It may take them time to overcome these feelings. Think carefully about who you tell and be considerate of their feelings also.

If you have been through a treatment programme for alcoholism, then you will already have had the experience of meeting lots of other people from very different backgrounds who have also shown that they feel the same way you do.

It can be enormously powerful to know that other people are frightened too, and see through them that a lot of fears are unreasonable or can be dealt with. If you haven't been to treatment yet I would urge you to at least attend a few Alcoholics Anonymous meetings, so you can hear other people talk about how they deal with their fears and how they have recovered.

What I am suggesting is that you begin to share how you feel with someone, somewhere. It will help enormously with dealing with your fears. When we begin to talk about them out loud they begin to lose their power over us.

Fear is entwined with everything. However, with some work on your part and continued sobriety, you will be amazed at what you can overcome. I was terrified of any social situation and couldn't believe that in sobriety I would ever be able to socialise again. But slowly, over time, I began to take small steps, and I found the fear was unwarranted and I overcame it. Years ago, the thought of going to a birthday party or celebration was terrifying to me. I had no idea how I would talk to anyone without the aid of alcohol. Now, I don't even think about it. I can socialise and talk to anyone, without a moment's fear. So start with small steps, share your fears with someone you trust, ask for help, challenge the thoughts, and gradually you will make progress.

Freedom in our minds

This is what every alcoholic has been looking for, whether they knew it or not. It wasn't until my mind became free that I realised what a toxic waste dump it had become. If we hold on to our guilt, shame, secrets, sadness or our haunted toxic thoughts, then we feel bad. If we feel bad for long enough then we will look for ways to change this, and in most cases we pick up our drug of choice.

Our minds can work against us, or for us. It all depends on how we treat them. Become aware of the thoughts that are dominating your thinking, especially if you have resentments against people for perceived injustices done to you. Recognise how you are fuelling these thoughts, and the price you are paying for allowing them to go over and over in your mind. It might help to write some of them down.

Renting space in your head

Think about this. Who and what do you rent free space in your mind to? And what does that do to you? *No one inhabits your thoughts unless you invite them in.*

We allow other people's actions to dominate us by constantly going over in our minds conversations and situations that have troubled us. When we get caught up in worrying what other people think about us we are giving away our personal power. We do this when we are dissatisfied and are dominated by what other people may or may not have done to us. We just can't seem to let 'it' go. By going over old resentments and frustrations we are 'chewing' on them, often making them worse than they actually were.

In sobriety we have to learn to let these things go. The 12 Steps of Alcoholics Anonymous is an excellent way of doing this. But you might also find Cognitive Behavioural Therapy (CBT) or other types of therapy equally useful. Creating order and peace in our thinking usually requires an outside intervention or help; as our own thinking created the problem, so a new of thinking is required for the solution.

But rest assured that the sober mind can be one that is free of resentments, anger and fear – this is what you are working towards. A free mind is the best insurance against drinking.

"The thoughts we choose to think are the tools we use to paint the canvas of our lives." Hay, 2004

Beliefs

Our belief system is one of the ways our fear, shame and guilt are fuelled. We form beliefs about ourselves, the world and other people from our early experiences. The process of how we understand these experiences is how we create meaning and make sense of the world.

Beliefs are created by the *interpretations* we put on events. These thoughts and ideas that become our beliefs are mostly unquestioned. We accept them as facts. We think they are black and white facts about how the world is and there is no changing them. We treat our beliefs as realities, as immoveable truths. Because they emanate from inside us, they have great power over us. They govern our lives when we don't challenge them.

In *Awaken the Giant Within*, Anthony Robbins discusses how our thoughts, expectations and actions originate from these beliefs. They have enormous power to shape the direction of our lives, and to make that experience positive or negative. Examining your beliefs is one of the most important things you can ever do.

Beliefs are our way of interpreting the world to make sense of it. Some of us do this in a way that is unhelpful to our growth and development as human beings. We form limiting beliefs. Common limiting beliefs are:
- I'm stupid.
- I'm unattractive.

- I'm fat.
- I'm useless.
- I can't change.
- I'm not as good as other people.
- I'm not good enough.
- No one will love me.
- If people really knew me they wouldn't like me.
- I might get found out.
- If something goes right for me something always comes along and messes it up.
- Rich people are lucky – I'd be OK if I had money.
- Everyone else seems to know what they're doing.
- Life is hard.

These limiting beliefs could be formed by experiences you had when you were young. I formed many limiting beliefs from experiences I had as a child and young adult. If I didn't get picked for something, or I felt rejected by friends, I always thought *'This is happening because I'm not good enough'.* Eventually, that became my truth; I just felt I wasn't good enough and my behaviour kept reinforcing the belief. It became a self-fulfilling prophecy.

I can guarantee that as an alcoholic you will have more than your fair share of limiting and negative beliefs. Our messy, damaging, chaotic alcoholic behaviour would have provided very fertile ground for limiting beliefs to take root and grow. By the end of my drinking my belief system was very negative; I believed everything about me was negative. It wasn't until I got sober that I finally began to challenge these beliefs and to my amazement found out they weren't true! Gradually, I began to change them and guess what? When I began to change my beliefs my experience of life began to change.

Imagine who you'd be if you believed different things about yourself. Have you ever stopped to question what you believe about yourself? What happens is that we become what we think. So if we believe we aren't good enough, that no one likes us and we are losers, then our experience of life will reflect these thoughts.

Our beliefs are a *filter system*. Therefore your brain will filter out anything that doesn't fit with the beliefs you have created. It only accepts and captures information that fits your model of the world. It's like a fishing net.

Many people can work through their limiting beliefs on their own, see how silly they are and dismiss them. Other people, however, can let them fester, and as they get older the beliefs become more significant. Every alcoholic I've ever worked with has had an extremely negative belief system. Over time, once they have got sober they have been able to challenge them and see themselves differently.

As an interesting exercise, cast your mind back over past incidents, particularly from your childhood and teenage years, and see if you can see them from a different angle. Is the meaning that you applied to the event absolutely true? How do you know? Can you look back at certain events and see that, actually, a different interpretation could be applied?

We can then go on and look at different events and turn them into positive beliefs. Sometimes when our minds are full of negative beliefs we actually don't notice the positive things right in front of us.

A negative belief could be: 'I'm such a loser. I've only been sober for two months. My life is a mess'. The negative belief is that 'I'm not good enough'.

Could a more positive belief be: 'I've been sober for two months. It's the hardest thing I've ever done. I've worked so hard to achieve this and slowly things are getting better. I'm turning my life around'. The positive belief is that 'I'm good enough. I'm brave, courageous, hard working, determined'.

Try to see how different positive beliefs make you feel. This is something you can practise over time. I wanted to bring your attention to how powerful beliefs are and how they impact our lives. The good news is that we have the power to change them if we choose to.

Healing our souls

Just like our physical bodies, our souls have been badly damaged by alcoholism too. This is why we must allow them time to heal. Healing will start as soon as you put down your last drink. Just like the body, your soul will start to heal when you just start treating it better. This chapter has covered many different ways you can start doing that.

Chapter 8

Relationships and Sobriety: Part I

We have to love ourselves first. That is our responsibility, not someone else's. All other healthy, mature love follows. By developing an understanding of our relationship patterns we can discover how healthy relationships work.

'VE DEDICATED TWO chapters to exploring relationships, because they are such a significant part of everyone's lives, whether they are with family members, friends or lovers. Relationships can be joyful and they can be devastating, and all things in between. They can be particularly challenging for the alcoholic, and for anyone who is in a relationship with an alcoholic. Romantic relationships have a particular precedence in our lives and seem to be the source of great consternation and pain as well as joy. Alcoholics are no different in this.

This chapter will begin to untangle the threads that create our relationships and allow you to get clarity and focus with the relationships that are important to you. It will also look closely at romantic relationships and how these can be transformed.

A successful, happy, loving, committed, passionate, exciting, dynamic relationship is possibly the hardest thing you will ever do. When I met my husband, he asked me on our first date if I could name five relationships that I envied. I could only name two. I could name dozens of relationships, but ones I actually envied? Who had something I wanted? Now that was hard. I'm not sure why that is. Is it because it's just not possible to have a successful, happy, loving, committed, passionate, exciting, dynamic relationship these days? Is it perhaps too much to ask? Or, are people just settling for second best; compromising, entering and maintaining relationships based on fear of loneliness?

I'm not sure I have all the answers, but I do know relationships are the hardest thing to do and I see that in everyone I know. Having a relationship, finding a relationship, losing a relationship, are the main topics of conversation for a lot of people. Sometimes the need for a relationship, and what we perceive it can offer us, means we stay in relationships that aren't good for us.

Unhealthy relationships

I could write a whole book on unhealthy relationships. I've had so many of them! After a lot of personal therapy and a lot of work on myself I finally became capable of healthy commitment. Relationships don't come easily to a lot of people, but it's even harder for people who drink. Add some alcohol abuse to a relationship and stand back and wait for the explosion.

All of my relationships whilst drinking were complete and utter disasters. In hindsight, all of my relationships were based on my misguided belief that the right person would fix me. If I had the right relationship, the right man, then everything would be perfect.

I was still focusing on external fixes at this point and it really didn't cross my mind that I was an insecure, manipulative, dishonest, frightened, needy, shallow, unmanageable, screwed-up mess, and that no right minded, decent, emotionally intelligent man would come within a hundred paces of me. I was convinced they'd see beyond all of that to the true beautiful soul that I was, and come charging through North London on their white charger, and further, that a single kiss from them would dissolve all of those glaring character defects. I was clearly living in fantasyland, a land I occupied with a lot of other people.

Instead of attracting the right man, I attracted a lot of wrong men. Because you see, emotionally healthy people are just not attracted to the kind of person I was. Unhealthy men, however, found me very attractive and I had endless pointless, insincere relationships, because frankly it was better than being on my own.

However, a relationship is never going to work when two love-starved and needy individuals demand the other person 'fix them'. I just had nothing to give. It was all about me, getting me fixed.

As I wasn't capable of having a healthy functioning relationship, I took 'hostages'. I grabbed on to someone and didn't let go, no matter what I thought or felt. I was just desperate not to be alone. So any willing victim would do. I 'engineered' all of my relationships. I was controlling and manipulative. Some of the men I had relationships with I cared for, but the truth was that they were never based on love. They were based on fear. Fear of:

- loneliness,
- not being loved
- being 'left on the shelf'.

And once *in* the relationship, the fear was of:

- not being good enough,
- being rejected,
- having them discover who I really was.

Plain old fear. Lots of it.

I found there were plenty of emotionally messed up men, who were more than happy to engage in this warped dance. I used sex to get love, and attracted men who used love to get sex. It's a game that men and women have been playing since time began.

Relationships in recovery can be equally hazardous, because without the security blanket of alcohol we are laid bare. We are exposed and we are most definitely frightened as hell. Romantic relationships key into our deepest fears of not being worthy of love. We are frightened of the other person getting too close, seeing who we really are and rejecting us, thus confirming what we believed in the first place – a faulty belief, by the way. So from the start we are unconsciously pushing the other person away and acting on this faulty belief and, in this way, we create this as our experience again and again. And thus the faulty belief is reinforced.

It's as though we have completely bought the fairy tale, and believe true love will solve all our problems, if only we could find it. All love stories end when the couple fall in love and kiss. This is the implied solution. Everything will be perfect now because love conquers all. But this is actually when the hard work really starts, because in reality 'our true love' is an imperfect human being who has their own emotional baggage, just as we do.

This was my pattern, and I see it in my clients all the time. It's the constant illusion that love from another person will make all the bad stuff go away. But the truth is that when you don't love yourself, or even like yourself, it's impossible to receive love from another person. We either destroy that love under the weight of our insecurities and fear, or we settle for second best because we are so scared of rejection or being alone, or worse, because we believe we don't deserve better.

In my early twenties I was in a relationship with a good man who adored me. He wanted to marry me and he offered me everything I had ever dreamed of. I didn't love him and I don't think I ever really fancied him. I could only sleep with him when I was drunk. Isn't that crazy? Why would anyone want to be in a relationship like that? It's obvious it's never going to work out, it's a recipe for disaster. The reason I was in it, and stayed in it, was because it was safe and I was so frightened. I stayed because I didn't know how to cope with the world. I stayed because that's what other people were doing: getting married, settling down. They seemed happy and I thought that if I did the same thing as they were doing, I would eventually be happy too. In my work as a therapist I've discovered I wasn't the only one.

Lucy's story

My drinking affected my relationships with everyone. The relationships that were most affected, where I caused the most upset and damage, were the ones with men that I was involved with, had been involved with or wanted to be involved with. My entire being was centred around men. I obsessed over them constantly and I used alcohol and drugs to obliterate any pain, any feelings that arose around relationships. It is not until I sobered up at thirty-one that I was able to stand still and actually look around me at the nuclear fall out and chaos that I had caused in my relentless pursuit of the 'perfect relationship': in my un-nerving and completely misguided belief that I could fill the paternal,

Dad-shaped hole in my world with a boyfriend, where I traded my worth for sexual currency.

In the daytime or the rare evenings when I wasn't drinking, I was obsessing and fantasising over one or more men. My entire waking hours would be spent attracting men to flirt with, 'maintaining' a relationship, or actively seeking a new one, often whilst in the death throes of an existing one. I attracted men using funny, feisty, overtly sexual and confident behaviour, and then when they were sufficiently hooked, I used my childhood backstory to show my vulnerable side and they would fall in love with me. After the thrill of the chase and the games in getting them to that point, I would then instantly become bored and would start the pattern again, outside the relationship. Sometimes this happened within days, sometimes it took years.

Whilst drinking I had sexual encounters with over fifty men and I cared little for my own sexual health, or theirs. I woke up next to strangers and in unknown beds on numerous occasions, always with the same tight throat, churning stomach and confused desperation – asking myself as I groped for my clothes 'How on earth did I do this again?'.

When I got into recovery, the sexually promiscuous behaviour stopped, with self-imposed abstinence, and then I fell in love around my one-year sober anniversary. At first I was convinced that all my Christmases had come at once and that the all-healing 'fix' had finally been delivered to my door. Instead of carefully nurturing and slowly developing this relationship, I threw myself headlong into a co-addicted, co-dependent partnership, with an intensity and fervour, the like of which I had never previously known. Once I had finally suffocated the life out of that love, it quickly became clear that the drinking had merely been a symptom of a far deeper and more lethal case of love addiction.

On my knees and suicidal yet again, desperately unhappy, and staring back into the abyss, I couldn't believe that after all the recovery work I had done I was in fact mentally more out of balance than before, and worse still, I couldn't medicate with alcohol or drugs. I had left holes in my recovery. Holes that I chose to studiously ignore. It wasn't until I fell into one of those holes that I found that they were in fact gaping chasms, and I couldn't climb out alone. After reaching out, I found another self-help group and accepted my newly unearthed addiction; then I began the long and incredibly intense recovery process of reaching out to God, and asking him to help me get back on my feet again.

Lucy, 33, sober since 2008

Recognising co-dependency

What Lucy is describing is co-dependency. Co-dependency is still relatively unrecognised in the UK as an illness, or mental health condition. In America, it is acknowledged as a legitimate condition that can have chronic and disabling effects on the sufferer. Melody Beattie, the author of *Codependent No More* and *Beyond Codependency*, was a pioneer in this field. Her work focused on how destructive co-dependency could be and how, in particular, it affected alcoholics and addicts. Co-dependency is not exclusive to alcoholics; it is a very common condition. Co-dependency, however, is often part of alcoholism. Alcoholics will often get into relationships with people who are non-addicted but severely co-dependent, because the latter can meet all their unhealthy needs.

In essence, co-dependents manage their feelings, identity and self-worth by trying to manage other people. Co-dependency is ultimately about controlling the environment around them so that they can control their own inner turmoil.

These are very powerful behavioural patterns and I see them around me all the time. These behaviours are often at the core of why a relationship isn't working. A co-dependent has no real autonomy over their emotional life. They often feel that they are at the mercy of the elements, so often feel very frightened and un-anchored. This can sometimes be traced back to an abandonment experience by a primary care-giver in their childhood. This experience, or rather the *interpretation* of this experience, can express itself in a fear of not being loved, or of losing love, or worst of all, a fear of not surviving if the source of love is removed. Thus, the co-dependent believes their survival, or their feeling of being 'OK', depends on controlling others in order to feel OK.

TYPE I

The co-dependent will expend an enormous amount of energy attempting to control people in their environment. They will lie, manipulate, blame and control others around them into being or doing what the co-dependent wants them to be or do. The motivation for this behaviour is that the co-dependent believes they will then be happy (safe), and the people around them will be happy too, (they just don't know it yet!).

Of course, this is a one-way street to disaster, as other people will *never* be how we want them to be. They will be how *they* want to be, because that is free will. Co-dependents will often end up feeling lonely, depressed, abandoned, disillusioned, frustrated, bitter and angry – all the feelings they were trying to avoid. They remain totally unaware that they are the originators of these feelings. They will always blame everyone else for how they feel; they have the expectation that others need to change in order for them to feel OK.

It can be a painful experience being in a relationship with someone who has these characteristics, because they try hard to make the world the way they think it should be. They twist themselves up in knots trying to live up to the co-dependent's standards, or to meet their needs. They will constantly feel like they have failed, as no matter how hard they try they never seem to be able to make the other happy. The co-dependent is always ultimately dissatisfied. Both parties are unhappy and frustrated. This cycle will repeat itself over and over.

TYPE II

The other way co-dependency can be expressed is when the co-dependent has no sense of 'self' and becomes whatever they believe others want them to be. They are chameleons, forever changing their outsides to suit who they are with. They lose themselves, and can make no decision or choice by their own volition. It is always to suit the person they are with – parent, friend or lover. They constantly feel desperate because they never feel good enough. They feel like failures because no matter how hard they try to be what they believe their significant other wants them to be, they always fail. Again, the motivation for this behaviour is that this type of co-dependent believes they will finally be happy or safe, once they have pleased or satisfied the people around them. They repeat this over and over, trying harder and harder each time.

In both types, the co-dependent is in a doomed dance.

Alcoholics and addicts can display both of these types of behaviour, and also be attracted to people who are co-dependent: each relying on the other to make them happy, and ultimately failing. The first step to overcoming co-dependent behaviour is to recognise it within yourself, then you can take steps to change it. I can happily report that, with some work, this behaviour can be overcome, and be replaced by healthy, happy relationships. With all the work I have done with alcoholics, I believe that co-dependency should never be ignored. In most cases, co-dependency is a problem right alongside the alcoholism. If this were recognised earlier, the chances of a sober alcoholic entering into an unhealthy relationship and relapsing could be minimised.

Relationships: our life task

The thing about human relationships is that they are always moving, changing and growing. They are organic in nature and just because we are in a relationship right now doesn't mean we always will be. They are a task we have to work at constantly. Different circumstances and events can have an impact on our committed relationships, as we learn new ways to respond to these changes. It's not just romantic relationships that we need to work on, but also relationships with our friends, families, colleagues and acquaintances. They can all be improved. This requires conscious effort on our part.

Identify your relationship patterns

If you look back over the last few years, what are the patterns you've 'acted out'?

Disapproval, abandonment, rejection, possessiveness, intensity followed by apathy? Are you a serial monogamist or a serial adulterer? Uncommitted/overcommitted? Look at all of your past relationships objectively and see if you can begin to identify a pattern of behaviour on your part.

By identifying our patterns we become more intelligent, more informed, more self-aware. When we wake up to ourselves and get honest we can see that we often *knew* what we were doing, we just *chose* not to acknowledge it. We lied to ourselves, and we did this because we were scared, scared we wouldn't be loved, so we clung onto relationships that weren't right for us.

Relationship baggage

Not only do we have to deal with the stuff from our family of origin, but we have to clear the wreckage from our past relationships too. All of our past relationships, no matter how bad they were, have great lessons that we can take from them and grow from. By doing this we then have a chance of creating the relationship we want, instead of just repeating the same pattern.

Many of us have a relationship pattern. This is the behaviour we repeat over and over again with different people. At first we might think it's the other person who's doing this to us, but in reality it's something we are doing. If we can *uncover* it, we can *change* it. It's much harder to keep on doing something when we see what it is we are doing that harms us.

My pattern in relationships was this: I would meet a guy who would be completely dazzled by me. He would pursue me and tell me how amazing, beautiful and incredible I was. We would have sex and I would think we were in a relationship. He would then become indifferent to me and eventually push me away, and I would be heartbroken.

This happened every time. And every time a little piece of me broke inside, to the point that I seriously considered a life of celibacy and aloneness, because I simply couldn't go through that level of pain again.

Of course, I was repeating the abandonment I had experienced from my father, but even knowing this didn't prevent me from continuing the pattern. By becoming spiritually fit I began to see that I attracted insecure men into my life who were at first very attracted to my confidence and exuberance – even when drinking I could come across this way. But because they felt so insecure with themselves, they couldn't handle my being this way, so they pushed me away. And because I used to interpret everything personally, I thought it was because I wasn't good enough. It came as a revelation to me that it wasn't because of me that they backed away. It was because of their own failings and inadequacy that they had to leave.

I also realised that I had been settling for kitchen boys, not princes. I was damn well good enough, but I had to see this first. And when I finally believed that, my behaviour changed accordingly. Through changing my behaviour, the results changed, and that is the reason I finally became someone who could give and receive love.

Common relationship mistakes

The key to having a healthy relationship is to recognise the reasons for going into it. If you're going into it for the wrong reasons then the result is usually an unhealthy relationship. If you have a pattern of unsatisfactory relationships, then it is important to look at your co-dependency issues. A common mistake is looking for someone to save you or fix you. Firstly, you are not broken so you don't need 'fixing', and secondly, by creating that belief system you give all your power away and take on the role of a pathetic victim.

Only children are victims, adults volunteer for the role.

Unconsciously, as adults, we start playing out the same pattern again and again. People *volunteer* to be victims in relationships, because this is all they are used to. They have learnt to be treated this way. This isn't their fault, as they don't know any better. However, at some point, as an adult, they have to stop and look at themselves, and take *responsibility* for changing. Nobody can fix you or save you, simply because no other human being has that kind of power. Only you can do that for yourself.

Behaving as a victim will attract two types of people. The first one believes their purpose in life is to find someone to 'fix' or 'save'. It's how they get their needs met and self-esteem raised, by becoming a 'rescuer'. Someone who has this belief system is often 'using' the person they are 'saving' in order to distract themselves from looking at their own issues. By allowing someone to save you, you 'give yourself away'.

The second type will be attracted to 'victims' they can abuse. Victims attract abusers like magnets.

The only way to have the relationship you want and deserve is to *become* the kind of person you want to have a relationship with, and then you will attract that person into your life. Like attracts like. Become the kind of person you want to attract.

Lola's story

At the age of twenty-three I hit rock bottom after a ten-year battle with binge drinking, starving myself, bingeing on vast amounts of food then purging. I entered treatment out of desperation to turn my life around. I was, for the first time in many years, compliant and teachable.

After a few months in recovery I was eating three meals a day, was abstinent from alcohol and all other mind altering chemicals (including the anti-depressants I had been on for years), and my self-esteem, which had been virtually non-existent, was building; through my willingness to be emotionally honest I was building priceless friendships with others.

My spirit was alive again and I felt as if I had returned to the enthusiastic, carefree place I had been in before my addictions took over. Family and friends were gaining confidence that I was getting better and were beginning to forgive my past behaviour.

After four years of continuous sobriety, I married my husband Matthew, also a recovered alcoholic. We were married a year when I woke up to the fact that our relationship was suffering. For trivial reasons, I would yell at him, slam doors and cry uncontrollably. I expected him to be how I wanted him to be, and blamed him for letting me down. I also became aware of the extent to which I had begun again to obsess about what others thought of me – a feature of active addiction and early recovery, which had tapered off. I would lie in bed running conversations over and over in my mind, convinced that because someone said something in a certain way, it meant that they didn't like me. I was desperate for the approval and validation of others. I sought help and quickly realised that love addiction had been at my very core and that I had used alcohol and food to medicate this very painful issue. I do believe, however, that I needed to stop my alcohol and food dependency before I could reach this truth about myself.

I took a long hard look at my history around relationships of all kinds. For as far back as I can remember I had been looking for a 'saviour'. Someone who would rescue and take care of me. I would put friends, teachers, counsellors and boyfriends on pedestals, and would be crushed if they let me down or disappointed me in any way. I believe that alcohol and food came in as more reliable 'saviours'. They always did what they promised to do – gave me a sense of ease and comfort, or oblivion – and they were more trustworthy than people.

So when the addictions to alcohol and food stopped, my addiction to people and their approval began to progress, until I reached a place where I could no longer deny the pain I felt in this area. I realised that I had been living for others: trying to work out what others expected of me and behaving accordingly, so that I would gain their approval and prevent them from leaving me. It was all an attempt to control the uncontrollable!

I knew this pattern had to stop. I was emotionally dependent on my husband and I couldn't bear the pain I was in around some of my friendships. I began to abstain from certain behaviours. I decided I should no longer seek approval from others, or use my husband as an emotional dumping ground. This took a lot of support from people who understood, because the habits of a lifetime were being broken. I didn't know if my marriage or friendships would survive and it was very frightening. But as a result of entering recovery from love addiction I can say that for the first time in my life I feel complete as a human being. I am whole, without the need for any approval or validation from others. I am grateful beyond words for knowing that there is no human power that could ever fulfil what I was searching for in life, yet there *is* a power that can do exactly that, and I can tap into it at any moment of any day – it is within.

Lola, 31, sober since 2004

About love

I do not profess to be anything of an expert in this area, especially with my own track record. I also know that a whole series of books could be written on this area alone, but I think it is worth including in a book about alcoholism.

Why? Because every alcoholic I have ever met craves love, yet does everything they can to destroy it. It evades us like the promise of a British summer. And they are right. Love is important. It really is all there is. It's how to go about it that throws so many people.

It is the human fantasy – every song, every play, every film, every book is about love of some description: the need for it, the destruction of it, the pursuit of it, the ending of it, the sheer joy of it, the life changing powers of it. It's all about love.

Love is the Holy Grail for nearly all human beings, and certainly as alcoholics and addicts we succumb to the false illusion that love from another human being will *save* us. The truth is that *nobody will love us until we can love ourselves.*

We teach people how to treat us, and if we think nothing of ourselves, then on an unconscious level others will pick up on this and treat us accordingly. If you don't love yourself, how do you expect anyone else to love you? Love can be so confusing sometimes, we can get lost. What is love? How do we know if it's real?

It's easier to answer what love is *not*:
- hurting deliberately
- smothering
- shaming
- dominating
- controlling
- blaming
- manipulating
- deceiving
- humiliating
- abusing
- oppressing
- denying

- punishing
- limiting
- hiding
- bullying.

People often get 'stuck' in very harmful relationships because of 'love'. Newsflash: *It's not love*. It's fear.

The best description I've ever heard of love was given by a seventy something recovered alcoholic Catholic nun; she described love like this: 'Love is someone who brings you life'. Not *a* life – but there is life in what they bring. Start by recognising what love is and what love *isn't*. Define it for yourself, then you will at least know what you are looking for.

Loving yourself first

The reason that we seek love in so many places is that love is essential to life. Eric Fromm in *The Art of Loving* talks about human beings experiencing 'separation anxiety', and because of this we seek love in other people, to ease the anxiety caused by knowing that we are alone.

Fromm uses this theory to explain why we are all so desperately seeking love and why, because of this, we often make inappropriate choices. He goes on to say that it is only by truly loving oneself that one can seek mutual love with someone else. This is the challenge for everyone, including the alcoholic. It would be safe to say that an alcoholic in early recovery is a long way from liking themselves, let alone loving themselves. But it is possible, with time.

So in order to receive love from others, we have to begin the journey of self-love. Starting to love yourself is much easier than it sounds. It starts with action. Just asking for help with an alcohol problem is, in fact, a great act of self-love. If you ask for help you must believe that you are worth something. It can continue from there. Eat a bit more healthily: that is loving the body. Do something you enjoy, that makes you smile: that is loving the soul. As long as we are still breathing, we still have the ability to give and receive love. Bit by bit, we can crawl out of the dark hole of aloneness and feel connected to the world again.

Chapter 9

Relationships and Sobriety: Part II

Alcoholic relationships can be very destructive and painful. If you are in a relationship with someone who is an alcoholic it can dramatically affect your own mental health and emotional wellbeing. Tough love may be the only answer to help someone who is still in denial. Alcoholics also need to consider their relationships with their families and peer groups.

Having a relationship with an alcoholic

IF YOU ARE reading this book because someone you love or are close to has a drink problem, then it's important to understand how you can minimise the impact of their drinking on your own life and happiness. You can also learn how changing your own reactions to their drinking can help and support them in their journey of recovery.

It's very tough to love someone who drinks. It's heart-breaking to stand on the sidelines, witnessing someone self-destruct, and be powerless to stop it. Alcoholism never just affects the person who is drinking. It affects everyone around them. It is a disease that can cause pain and misery to many people. Depending on the type of relationship, it can affect people in different ways.

Many alcoholics were children of alcoholics themselves. If you are a child of an alcoholic this can have a huge impact on how you perceive yourself and the world around you. Growing up with a parent who drinks means that a child will always come to the conclusion that their parent loved booze more than they loved the child.

My husband Rob grew up with an alcoholic mother, who died when he was eight years-old. He remembers his mother wanting to take him and his younger brother to Disneyland. They were so excited, as little kids are at the thought of meeting Mickey and his friends. When they got to the airport in San Francisco, their mother went straight to the bar. Rob and his brother played quietly as they waited for boarding to be announced. Their mother kept drinking at the bar and when she tried to get up off her stool she fell over and split her head open and had to be taken to hospital. The boys never went to Disneyland and a dream was shattered. Can you imagine the feelings of disappointment and rejection they would have felt? Not to mention that yet again their mother had ruined something that was meant to be special for them.

What conclusions would they draw from this? That they weren't special, or worth anything because their own mother never put their needs first? This happens to children all over the world. Children don't need to go to Disneyland to feel special, they just need to know that they are loved and central to their parent's lives. It's not telling your children you love them, it's *showing* them, that counts. Rob's mum might have woken up the next day and said she loved her boys a hundred times over, but it would have been worthless to them because she couldn't *show* them. Her actions showed them that she chose booze over them.

The hardest thing for a young child to do is to understand that their parents' behaviour is separate from them. We interpret behaviour *personally,* so that when a parent is 'unavailable' to a child because their attention is consumed by alcohol and their own suffering, then the child is going to come to the conclusion that they are not loved, or that they are not good enough. They start to believe that the parent's behaviour is somehow *their fault.* They feel responsible for their parent's drinking and start to believe that if they tried harder, maybe they could win the parent's love.

This can set a pattern that can continue into their adult life, and can cause emotional trauma and problems in their romantic relationships. Our relationship with our opposite sex parent sets up our patterns in our adult romantic relationships. The little boy whose mother was an alcoholic may look for a woman he can 'rescue', to try to heal the wound of not being able to 'rescue' his mother. Or, he may be unable to trust women. He may crave love, affection and intimacy, but never really be able to trust the woman giving it, so will always push her away, in the same way he felt his mother push him away.

The first significant love relationship we have is with our mother or father and if it was a painful relationship we are then prone to repeat this pattern in adulthood. What we are trying to do is to heal the pain of the original relationship by creating a different outcome. However, what often happens if we have experienced abandonment, rejection, enmeshment or lack of interest, is that we tend to recreate this in our romantic relationships, so the wound gets deeper and deeper.

With a bit of work this can be overcome, and it's important to start by recognising the impact that a parent's drinking had on you. First, it is vital to understand that their alcoholism never had anything to do with you, and you couldn't have stopped it or saved them.

It's similar if you are the parent of an alcoholic. The same principle applies. You need to separate your child's drinking from yourself. Parents often beat themselves up and blame themselves if a child is drinking or using drugs. No one is a perfect parent. Everyone makes mistakes and it's what you do now that matters.

If you have just got sober and are also a parent, then there is still time to make it up to your children. It is never too late. I have seen this so many times with clients. Families who seem broken beyond repair have become healed. As long as the alcoholic stays sober, then anything is possible.

Relationships with active alcoholics

Being in a romantic relationship with an alcoholic is also very difficult, especially if you fell in love and the drinking then crept up. You can end up with someone you no longer recognise. It is difficult, as you may often see the real person one day and then the next they are completely different and unreachable. When we love someone we stand by them. We want to help them. We want to love them better, but sometimes this isn't enough, and it's the people closest to the alcoholic who can help them the least. You can't 'love' an alcoholic better. But you can love yourself enough to have some boundaries around their behaviour. Remember, it may not be their fault they became an alcoholic, but it is their responsibility that they do something about it. It is also not *your* responsibility to do something about it.

I would encourage anyone who is in a relationship with an alcoholic to seek help independently, to support themselves and work through their feelings towards the drinker. Just being in a relationship with someone who is that emotionally ill can affect the emotional wellbeing of those closest to them.

Over a significant period of time the non-drinker can become as 'ill' as the drinker, as their sense of self and personal boundaries become lost in their desire to 'fix' the alcoholic. This behaviour in itself becomes unhealthy, as they no longer focus on their own needs or feelings. They detach from their own emotional guidance system and fixate on the alcoholic's feelings as their own indicator of how they should feel. Incredibly, there is a way to be happy and content whilst still in a relationship – of some kind – with an alcoholic. However, it is dependent on the concerned other person establishing emotional wellbeing in themselves first.

Carrie was in an alcoholic relationship for a long time. She didn't realise how crazy her behaviour had become until she finally found the strength to leave.

Carrie's story

My name is Carrie and my ex-husband was an alcoholic. Whilst I was with my husband I lived with fear, uncertainty and despair. I never knew from day to day what was going to happen. When he was drinking, my husband was very unreliable and lied all the time; he would let me down time and time again.

I was pregnant with my second child and ten days overdue when my husband decided to go out for a drink. He didn't come home that night; he arrived home at 6am in the morning, and without a word went straight to work.

That evening I went into labour. My husband was nowhere to be found so I drove myself to the hospital. When I arrived at the hospital the baby was in distress. I lay on the bed with monitors attached to me, listening to the heartbeat of my unborn baby, not knowing whether he would live or die. At that time I didn't see it as a big deal, it was what I was used to, but since being in recovery I've realised how traumatic that situation was for me, and that having no support from my husband was very difficult.

I felt like I was on a roller coaster ride, up and down all the time. I didn't have a life, my whole focus was on my husband and what he was doing, how much he was drinking, and who he was with. During our marriage my husband had affairs; I was always checking his pockets, his phone and wallet. There was no trust, but I would ask him to leave, then would always take him back. Our financial situation was dreadful because my husband would spend so much money on drink, and other things. I would borrow money from family so I could pay bills. I was always worried and we nearly lost our home.

I joined Al-Anon in June 1997, a fellowship for family and friends of alcoholics. I really didn't want to be in a room full of people that I didn't know and was very angry at the fact that I had to be there, but I found it very welcoming and I could identify with what people were saying.

I had neglected my children emotionally because my head was always with my husband, so I wasn't actually present for my children. On occasions, my husband would be very aggressive and violent; he would do things like pull my hair, push, poke and pinch me, then he started to get aggressive with my eight year-old son. I was too frightened to say anything because he was angry and always said he was right. Then one evening he told me he was going to talk to someone about a job. He didn't come home all night. The next morning I was taking my son for a scan to see if he had a brain tumour, and again my husband was not there to support me. It was then I decided that my children and I could no longer live in this situation. When he came home the following evening, I asked him to leave, and with the help and support of Al-Anon I was able to stay firm with my decision. For weeks and months afterwards my husband would beg me to take him back, crying, threatening to kill himself and me, but I never changed my mind.

I divorced my husband after being in Al-Anon for a year. I also looked at my part in the situation and learnt a lot about myself: about the choices I had made and how my self-esteem was so low that I put up with unacceptable behaviour, and how my own behaviour was also insane.

Since being in recovery my life has changed immeasurably. I have freedom, and today I have the tools to deal with life. I have a voice, which I never had; I am able to say 'No'. I like myself now. My children have also benefited a great deal, they have self-awareness and they are so much happier now. Also, they know that if they have a problem I am there for them.

Carrie, 49, member of Al-Anon for 15 years

Carrie is in a recovery programme called Al-Anon*, which is for people who are, or have been, in relationships with alcoholics. Although she never had an alcohol problem herself, she needed help because she had become so emotionally unwell from being in a relationship with an active alcoholic. She was able to deal with her relationship, and the unhealthy behaviour on both sides, because she finally found the strength to love herself. Getting out of this relationship was about survival for her. Her ex-husband is still drinking, still irresponsible, and very rarely sees his children or grandson, whereas Carrie is very close to her two children, who adore her. She has a full social life with lots of friends, and has finally fallen in love with a man who is worthy of her.

Leaving an unhealthy relationship is not the answer for everyone. Sometimes you may have to leave temporarily for the alcoholic to get better. Carrie had made the decision that her husband was choosing not to change, and could see nothing wrong with his behaviour. However, in

---

* Al-Anon is a 12-step self-help fellowship that supports the loved ones of someone with an alcohol problem. Like Alcoholics Anonymous, more experienced members offer help based on their experience of how the 12-steps work. See *www.al-anonuk. org.uk or www.al-anon.alateen.org* for further information.

many cases the relationship becomes stronger and better once the alco-holic decides to get help.

Healing past relationships: parents

Whether we had a good or bad experience growing up, our parents have a profound and long lasting impact on our lives, often without our realising. We will always be their child, no matter how old we are, and our task is to become independent of them: free of their baggage, which we inad-vertently picked up.

Even if your parents were absent, you will still have to deal with your ex-perience of not being parented adequately. Co-dependency can often occur in adult and child relationships, and can continue into the child's adult life.

Without realising it, parents can convey strong messages: that the child needs to please the parents in order to receive their love, or that the child exists to provide the parent with the love they never received. This can be when the seeds of co-dependency are planted. We can grow into adults who are never free of the unhealthy chains that bind us to our parents' approval. Often, our parents don't realise what they are doing, and may never recognise their behaviour, so we have to be responsible for 'unchaining' ourselves.

The words *mother* and *father* are two of the most powerful words we have in our vocabulary, and are usually the first words we learn. They are powerful because of the *meanings* we attach to them. The word 'mother' in our culture generally means: love, comfort, support, tenderness, safety, gentleness, caring etc. The word 'father' in our culture generally means: discipline, order, authority, power, fun, guidance, leader, etc. When you take these words away from the person, all you have left *is* a person who is trying to do the best they can, however inadequate that may actually be.

The words 'Mum' and 'Dad' are powerful because of these mean-ings; we project onto them an image of perfection. No one can live up to what the word suggests. Like you, mums and dads are works in progress.

So, one of the keys to freedom is to let go of your parents, and what they did and didn't do to you. They are just people after all. Have a relationship with them, but stop getting angry or frustrated with them. Stop blaming them. You only keep yourself chained if you don't.

Now here's the deal: your parents are human beings too and they were doing the best they could with the tools they had available. All their behaviour was about them, and not you. This is very important. The way your parents behaved didn't have anything to do with their loving you or not loving you.

This stuff can be very complicated, not to mention painful, so I'll try to make it as simple as possible. At some point, we do have to 'let go' of our parents. You may have had an absent or abusive parent – sexually, mentally, emotionally or physically – or an inadequate parent. You may have had a parent who wasn't fully 'present' because they were so wrapped up in themselves. You may have had a parent who couldn't express love. It's important that you know that *these were their failings, not yours*!

Abuse of any kind, especially by a parent, is a terrible thing. However, it wasn't your fault, and it certainly wasn't because you weren't good enough. However, this is the interpretation we come to, because when we are children we take everything personally. In fact, as adults we also take everything personally. We interpret the world personally. We interpret everyone else's behaviour to mean something personal, *especially* that of our parents. Knowing this is enormously freeing. Our parents were caught up in their own 'stuff', which sometimes had an impact on you.

So now it's time to see your parents as the flawed human beings they are. There's nothing bad about that; maybe they worked on themselves, maybe they didn't. Whatever their failings were, don't take responsibility for them. They're not yours. Put them down and experience what it's like to be free from that baggage.

We pick up lots of unwanted stuff from our parents: guilt, shame, feelings of not being good enough and so on. Now is the time to recognise this: *'uncover, discover, discard'*.

Learning from our families

Next, we need to examine how we learnt from our families. In our families we learnt how to use a knife and fork, how to talk, how to play etc. We also learnt how to do love, anger, blame, guilt, shame and so on, except that we learnt these things implicitly. They are rarely spoken about directly. We learnt through observation. We *observed* how our parents did these emotions and we copied them.

How did your parents 'do' love?

How did your parents 'do' anger?

How did your family 'do' feelings?

It's important to examine these things because we are mostly operating on someone else's way of experiencing the world and not our own.

My family, for instance, don't 'do' feelings. Feelings are rarely talked about and if they are, it's only 'safe' feelings that are tiptoed around. Nobody talks about hurting, struggling, grieving or being frightened or not coping. Any suggestion of these feelings and the atmosphere immediately becomes oppressive and suffocating. How do they do that? When I was younger, if I ever remotely broached one of these areas, I would get alarm bells going off in my head, transmitted by my mother's and aunts' tight faces and sharp intakes of breath.

My grandfather had died before I was born and I remember my cousins and I were always told in stage whispers, 'Don't talk to Nanny about Granddad!'. We were told not to talk about an upsetting subject because it would upset my grandmother. This was over twenty years after he had died. Children naturally want to learn and know things. We didn't want to hurt our grandmother, we wanted to share in her life. But my family had a strict rule of not talking about anything upsetting, and we had to follow it.

So I grew up in a family where I suppressed upsetting feelings because I was sent implicit messages that certain subjects weren't safe to talk about. Everyone pretended they weren't feeling what they were in fact feeling. I thought this was utterly bizarre. I felt like there was a huge secret that we weren't allowed to talk about for fear the earth would explode or something equally awful would happen. And so I learnt through my family: *never talk about how you really feel*.

A faulty rule – 'Thou must never truthfully express an emotion' – had been created through this experience, that for years I didn't question. Except of course, one day I realised that it didn't work for me, but then I nearly died through not understanding or being able to communicate how I felt. My feelings were a time bomb waiting to go off and I found that only large quantities of drugs and booze kept the lid on them.

In order to survive I had to learn how to 'do' feelings. So now I 'do' feelings, which is probably why I'm a therapist. I'm not advocating that we all need to go into therapy and talk about our parental relationships for hours, although some of us indeed might need to. What I'm suggesting is that you begin by reflecting on the messages you were given whilst growing up and ask yourself: 'Is this true?' 'Is this serving me?' 'Who taught me this?'. By asking these questions you may begin to undo another layer of faulty thinking and beliefs that your alcoholism has taken root in.

Show me your peer group and I'll show you your life

Peer groups are very interesting. They are, simply, the people we surround ourselves with: the people you spend the most time with, including your family, friends, colleagues, and in particular, the people with whom you drink.

Peer groups reflect back to us who we are. My peer group, when I was drinking, was mostly people who were just the same as me. To be honest, I didn't even like most of them. I just pretended I did. Some of my 'friendships' were based on fear of being alone, and they were just with people to do 'stuff' with, so I could convince myself I wasn't a 'lonely loser'. Others were with people I used for my own purposes, and other people were 'fair weather friends' at best. Nearly all my relationships felt uncomfortable or 'icky'. They never felt completely truthful or genuine. There were always hidden agendas in my friendships.

Abusing alcohol and drugs was the basis of most of my relationships. I drank and used drugs with people who drank and used in the same way I did. We colluded with each other. I justified my behaviour through theirs. My peer group was mostly full of insincere, selfish, insecure, shallow, manipulative people – because that's who I was.

However, I was also lucky that I did have some genuine friends who saw something in me that I couldn't see. Their friendship kept me alive. By some miracle these people stayed in my life and are my dearest friends today. They saw past my crazy behaviour to the real me and loved me despite that behaviour. I was an inconsistent and unreliable friend, but somehow they persevered with me. I remember from time to time meeting people who were genuine, interesting and authentic. I found these people very attractive and tried to form friendships with them. However, because I was insecure and frightened, not to mention chaotic and unreliable, I usually destroyed these friendships or pushed the people away because I was so ashamed or embarrassed about who I'd become. I never wanted anyone to get close. That's why my friendships were always changing. My sole criterion for friendship was, 'Did they drink? And did they drink the way I did?'. If so, then I could spend time with them. When I got sober I had very few friends left. The longer I stayed sober the more I knew that I couldn't risk hanging out with people who drank the way I used to.

Getting sober *may* mean changing your peer group. This isn't something you necessarily have to do consciously. When I stopped drinking, my social life stopped dead in its tracks. All my friends were fair weather drinking friends. I realised we had nothing in common and it was really too uncomfortable for us to see each other. As I began to become emotionally well, my peer group changed very naturally and I began to attract people into my life with whom I had always wanted to be friends, but had always been too scared of in the past. I attracted people who saw the world as I did, who had a curious mind, who had a thirst for life, who wanted to live their lives to the full. *People who lived their truth. People who weren't perfect, but who were always striving to be the best version of themselves they were capable of being.*

Now, my relationships feel genuine. I don't feel uncomfortable and I don't have to hide anymore. I can be honest and reveal my true self, imperfections and all, with no fear, because I know I am loved and accepted. My peer group lift me up. They celebrate my successes and support me in my challenges, and they inspire me and guide me. I am truly honoured and blessed to attract such incredible people into my life.

When someone within a peer group changes, it upsets the balance of the group. People generally don't like change. If you are part of a peer group which drinks like you do it will disturb them greatly if you stop. This is because you have stopped reflecting back to them who they are and are now reflecting back something they may not want to see yet. It's not uncommon for a peer group to try to influence someone by telling them they can't be an alcoholic and that they don't drink enough for that to be true – just remember that it's nothing to do with how much you drink. You may be frightened that they will laugh or ridicule you for getting help.

Remember who is sleeping in your head. You are not *them.*

Your peer group will be uncomfortable when someone changes; they may not be ready to change yet – certainly they don't *have* to, they are free to live their lives as pleases them – so a peer group may try to get you to change *back* to how you were because it's easier for *them*. This is because by getting *sober* you've upset the apple cart.

We need other people around us, but choose wisely who is going to accompany you on your journey through life.

I hope this chapter has helped you identify some areas in your life that you need to work on in order to maintain your sobriety.

If you are the loved one of an alcoholic I hope this chapter has provided you with some hope that things can change and improve, regardless of what happens to the alcoholic you love.

Chapter 10

Becoming the best version of yourself you are capable of being

Recovery from alcoholism is about you becoming the best you possible. So, treat yourself with love and respect; pay attention to how you are making choices and you will finally be free.

PART OF THE reason I wanted to write this book was to dispel the myth that getting sober means your life is over, and that you have to resign yourself to boredom and blandness. Nothing could be further from the truth.

Life without drink is far from boring. It is in fact, just the opposite. Believing a life without alcohol would be seriously 'less than' is a limiting belief that we tell ourselves in order to continue drinking. It's part of the denial. This final chapter explores some of the ways we can continue to improve our lives, and become the best version of ourselves we are capable of being now we are sober.

For ordinary people, alcohol can certainly be a means to have fun and relax. For alcoholics, the fun part stopped a long time ago. At the end of my drinking, about one time in a hundred was fun. I kept trying to drink the way I used to do at the beginning, when it was still new and exciting, but those days never came back. It was the same bars, with the same people, doing the same things, with the same results. Or it was drinking on my own, because I was bored or lonely. Towards the end, it was a lot more on my own.

My problem was that I just couldn't see a world without alcohol in it. I particularly couldn't see a way of ever socialising without it, and the thought of dating (let alone having sex!) was terrifying. And yet, all of those fears proved to be unfounded. I learnt to do all of those things, better, more authentically.

In the first six months of my sobriety, I steered well clear of bars, pubs and nightclubs. I was too scared to go into one. I wasn't just scared of drinking, I simply didn't know how to behave in those places without alcohol. So as I had no business being there, I didn't go. Instead, I hung out with other sober alcoholics and went for coffee and to the movies. This passed the time in the beginning. I felt safe and that was really all I wanted. I worked, and I focused on staying sober.

Before I knew it, my life opened up. Opportunities came my way that I could seize upon, instead of letting them pass me by. My social life opened up and I found that there was this whole world of things to do that I'd always missed out on because I was drunk or hung over. My confidence came back and I was able to talk to people sober. Eventually, I could go out dancing and socialise in places that served alcohol without thinking twice about it.

My life was now in Technicolor, whereas before it had been grey. The only way to describe it is that it was a re-birth. I'd realised that in my previous life I had been 'treading water'. Not living, just surviving. The thing that killed me the most in my alcoholism was that I knew I wasn't fulfilling my potential. I knew my life wasn't the way it was supposed to be. I knew I could be a better version of myself than I was. I just didn't know how to do it.

This is why getting sober isn't remotely boring. My life before was lived at 50% capacity at best. It is now a 100% life. Not perfect, but 100% authentic.

Jason's story

Beginning with my junior year in college, I had begun to drink alcohol and experiment with drugs. To most people, including myself, I was fully functioning in normal life, but I happened to be an alcoholic. I was told I had great potential and had experienced success academically, personally and professionally. Yet tragically I would throw each success away at the drop of a hat. From as far back as I can remember I had always felt different from other people. Alone. I hated and outright loathed myself. I played the victim in every aspect of my life, and I believed this lie with every fibre of my consciousness. I was gripped with fear of literally everything – people, places and things. My whole life I had been afraid to show people who I really was, to tell anyone how I really felt, who I really wanted to be, and what I really liked and loved.

After living with these feelings for twenty years, I found alcohol. And like a miracle drug, alcohol took these feelings away, if only for the moment. It was the key I had been looking for to make all these feelings disappear, even though it was only a fleeting relief. That was the beginning of an almost thirty year love affair I had with booze. It was my answer, my secret weapon, my buddy and pal. It was my trusted and closest friend. And then my friend started to turn on me.

Almost overnight after the first drink I suffered bad, sometimes terrible and tragic, consequences from drinking alcohol. But I still wouldn't quit and later arrived at the stage of alcoholism where I couldn't quit drinking on my own. My life was progressively getting worse at an exponential rate. Fights, 'Driving under the Influence', fired and jail, just to name a few of the consequences throughout my drinking career. I didn't want to die, but I also knew I couldn't continue living like this. I wasn't physically putting bullets in the gun, but metaphorically I was. I was committing suicide while playing the victim in my sad and tragic play by literally drinking myself to death. I was finally fired from my last job and had hit my rock bottom.

I have been sober since that day and haven't looked back. I found out I was suffering from a spiritual malady from which one can recover. I have found the peace and contentment of which I only dreamed, or saw others possess, much to my confusion and envy. I now have real relationships and friendships, even repairing some of the old damaged ones. I experience the laughter, love and light every day that I thought existed only for other people. I have confidence that is tempered with humility and gratitude. Many of the old opportunities that I had so easily tossed aside in my youth and alcoholism, as well as many new ones, present themselves in my life frequently. I am becoming the man I always wanted to be, the real me, the person I was afraid to show to the world my whole life: the authentic me.

Jason, 52, sober since 2008

This is what sobriety is all about. It's a way of living that we can't possibly have imagined before, and yet here it is.

Observe how you think and speak about yourself

As you grow in your recovery, there are lots of different tools you can use to enhance the quality of your sobriety. One of them is to pay attention to your thoughts, particularly the language you use to describe yourself. Quite frankly, if anyone else spoke to you the way you spoke to yourself, you'd punch them on the nose.

I have a challenge for you. Spend the rest of the day observing how you think and speak about yourself. My guess is you'll be shocked. We treat ourselves terribly! We are so harsh and mean to ourselves. We are un-accepting and punishing. We feel terrible about all these terrible things we say to ourselves; they're not true by the way, they just come from our faulty belief system. And the worst thing is: we are doing it to ourselves. No one else is doing it to us. How mad is that?

So stop. Stop being so awful to yourself. Every time you find yourself running that dialogue in your head: 'I'm so useless', 'I'm so fat', 'I'm so stupid' etc, stop. Pause. Breathe. Ask yourself, 'Is it absolutely necessary to speak to myself in this way? Could I perhaps be a bit kinder?'.

What we are doing by indulging in this negative self-talk is reinforcing all of our negative beliefs about ourselves. This is how we continue these beliefs and turn them into self-fulfilling prophecies.

You do this to *yourself.* No one does it to you.

This is good news, because you also have the power to stop it. Talking to yourself in such a terrible way is old alcoholic behaviour that kept you stuck in the dark hole of drinking. By paying attention to your thoughts a little more, instead of letting them just run through your mind, you can see how unnecessary it is to talk to yourself in this way. You are not a terrible person. You never were. You were an alcoholic and now you are sober. Start telling a different story.

Now you are awake – pay attention!

You are now fully responsible for your life and what you experience. You are also surrounded by teachers. Pay attention to the people around you. You will come across teachers who will show you how *not* to live your life and teachers who can show you how to live the life you want. All you need to do is to do what they do.

Neuro-Linguistic Programming teaches that 'modelling' is a very effective way of achieving the results you desire. It suggests that if you simply model someone else's success formula you will get the results they are getting. Success can be replicated.

This isn't about 'copying' someone else. It's about *learning* strategies to get the results you want.

Look closely at someone around you who has a life of failure and misery – what is it they do? I'd bet that a lot of what they do is bound up in their attitude to life and their beliefs about themselves. I'd bet they have lots of excuses and they blame their circumstances. I also suspect they self-sabotage a lot, too. From the outside looking in, it's very easy to see some-one else's mistakes and know what it is they should have done differently.

However, if you choose as a role model someone who is successful, it is a lot easier to be successful yourself. Once I was sober I was able to pay attention a lot more to what was going on around me. I noticed that to my surprise not everyone drank alcohol, in fact lots of people didn't drink or drank very minimally. I, of course, had thought everyone drank. It was enlightening for me to see how other people conducted their lives without alcohol, how they filled their lives, what they achieved. I had new teachers.

We have to accept that we don't know everything, that there are different methods of getting the results we want. We have to be humble enough to remain teachable, to accept that there is always more to learn. And remember, our minds are always limited by what we think we know. Accept that you know little. Look around for every opportunity to learn more. Don't spend your life looking down at the ground, look around you, get curious, pay attention.

What happens when we incorporate someone else's successful model into our own life? We make it our own. It becomes authentic. We don't become someone else. We become the people we were meant to be *all along*.

That's how I got sober. I completely accepted that I didn't know how to live life on any level because the results I was getting spoke for themselves: I was miserable, lonely, defeated. So I just did what someone else did in order to stop drinking and to change. I emulated them. Then I looked for role models in all the areas I wanted to improve: in my professional life, my dating life, my financial life and so on. And I got better results.

Listen more

In order to be able to successfully pay attention to what is happening around us we need to still our 'inner noise', to quieten our minds. We learn when we listen more. Have you ever had that experience of talking to someone who you know is not listening? Most people aren't listening, they are pretending to listen. They are just listening to noise inside their minds. They are distracted. Listening is an art, a skill, something we can learn and practise for the rest of our lives. It quietens the mind and, with practice, it brings internal peace and enables better communication.

Listen:
- without judging
- without criticising
- without thinking.

My spiritual mentor taught me these principles. He is a very good listener. When he listens you know you are being heard, and something funny happens when you know you are being truly listened to. You become more precise with your words. You find yourself articulating what you really want to say instead of just filling the air with random noise and babble. Being listened to is a very generous and humbling experience as it really makes you *think* about what you're saying. You become clearer in your thoughts.

It's true that we don't know what we know until we say it out loud. So speaking to someone who is generous enough to really listen enables the speaker to know themselves better.

We all know someone who uses ten sentences to say what really could have been said in two. They are stuck in their 'story'. They are not communicating. They are repeating their story. It reassures them. So practise listening.

You will find, astonishingly perhaps, that many conversations you have are not about communicating or sharing at all! Some people have no interest in what you think or what you have to say. They are only interested in having a 'body' to talk 'at'. It can be quite liberating to know that nothing is required from you, just your attention.

You'll find that by really listening, your conversations with people who are also able to listen and communicate will become much deeper, more meaningful, richer. Connections will be made at a much deeper, more intuitive level. Authentic communication with another human being is a gift, a joy to be cherished. It's where two souls meet and honour each other.

Start telling a different story

In addition to listening, notice what 'stories' you tell others. We sometimes get 'stuck', just telling the same story over and over again about why things haven't worked out, or why you feel let down, or all the terrible things that have happened to you. It's true that you can't change what happened to you, but you can choose your response to it. This is where you get your power back. If you were abused in some way as a child, if you were neglected or someone wronged you, these are terrible events. You had no part in creating them, but you do have a part in choosing how you react to them.

It may be true that terrible things have happened to you, but if you keep telling the story over and over again you are making your past your present. The present is unwritten...

People use their 'stories' to defend themselves. They are a defence against change, 'Look, see? If you had my story you would be a mess too!'. It's not true. Your past does not have to be your future, no matter how bad your past actually was.

In my work as a therapist I have heard some terrible stories from people's pasts: sexual abuse, violence, abandonment, rape, you name it, I've heard it. And I have seen some of these people rise above their circumstances and become the better version of themselves. So change the story from your past to one that empowers you to change. That no matter what you have been through, you are overcoming. You can create your own future; you have choice and you have power: when you change your 'story', you can change the outcome. This is no one's responsibility but yours.

Practise acceptance of others

We have explored how we change our inner world, but what can we do about our outer world – the one where we have to deal with other people and how they affect us? This is a challenge in itself, and very important for alcoholics, who can easily get caught up with other people's dramas and be affected by their behaviour. In my experience there is really only one way to deal with other people, and it is by accepting them as they are, not as we would have them be. It is something I continue to practise every day, especially with the people closest to me.

Acceptance of others is really the only way to have peace. We can't change people. We can't get them to do what we want them to do, when we want them to do it. They just won't. They just do what *they* want to do, how *they* want to do it.

But it can drive a person crazy, constantly running around trying to get the world to behave as they wish it would. I don't mean that we should sit by and passively accept behaviour that is clearly unacceptable. If someone is abusive, for example, we can't just accept that. We can remove ourselves from that experience and we should use whatever lawful means are necessary to ensure that the behaviour isn't continued.

The point I am making here is that we don't have to tolerate what is unacceptable, although we can accept that a person or circumstance may not change. What we can't afford to do is get twisted up in knots about it. Once we have accepted that the person may not change, we are *free* of the person and the behaviour. This is the goal of accepting others as they are. We become free from them. When we are trying to change them we are enslaved by them.

If I'm OK with me, I don't have to make you wrong.

This is what it boils down to. If I can't accept you just the way you are, it's usually because there is something wrong with me. I'd prefer *you* to change rather than to change myself because, frankly, that's easier. Most problems are caused because so many people are interfering with other people's behaviour. They don't like 'how they're doing it'.

Apply this in particular to your immediate family. You love them, right, but don't they drive you crazy with their behaviour? Can't they see that if they just saw things your way, or did things your way, everything would be so much easier? But it never works, does it? What usually happens when we try to sort out the world is that the world starts behaving even more badly than it did before, resulting in our feeling frustrated and resentful. Just imagine if you stopped focusing on other people's faults, and only focused on your own self-improvement. *And everyone else did the same...*

Practise accepting them – see what happens – see how you *feel*.

What we feed our minds is very important

We usually pay very little attention to what we feed our minds, which is shocking when we consider how vital our thoughts are. We are of course surrounded by easy to consume 'mental junk-food': the TV, the radio, the magazine shelf, commercials. All of this is fast food for the mind. It has no nutrients or healthy qualities. It just momentarily dulls the mind, like a Big Mac momentarily dulls the appetite; it's food sedation.

We unfortunately live in a culture where there is a saturation of shallow, meaningless, damaging 'mind-food'. It is very seductive and very easy to fill time up with, which is why we must be vigilant and we must be responsible for what we feed our minds on. Just like a diet of junk food will make us physically unwell, a diet of mind-junk food will make us spiritually and emotionally unwell. In fact it makes us quite sick.

I used to buy lots of women's magazines. I loved the fashion and the gossip, but over time I realised that the way women were treated by the media no longer sat comfortably with me. One page jeered at someone for being too fat, the other criticised someone for being too skinny. The articles were very judgemental and spiteful. It just didn't feel right. So I stopped buying them because I realised I couldn't participate in this behaviour any longer. It felt dirty. I'm no saint but I just found that as I became fully conscious I didn't like myself if I continued spending my time and filling up the space in my head with this pointless fluff.

The key is to be alert and aware, to let your mind absorb something that enriches and enlightens you. *Choose* what goes in. By all means watch TV, but switch it on to watch a programme that enriches you, then turn it off and have a conversation with someone. Don't sit there like a zombie for four hours, hypnotised by junk. Be responsible, your inner life is so precious, be conscious of how you use it.

Own your specialness

Whenever I look at my son I am filled with pride and love for him. He is so amazingly special to me, the most special little boy in the world. Of course most parents feel this way about their child, it's normal to feel this way.

Even if we weren't parented well, at some point *somebody* looked at us and thought we were special when we were children too. Then something happens and we become adults. We discover an unwritten rule that says we are no longer *allowed* to believe we are special, and worst of all, we dread anyone else thinking we could *think* we were special. That would be arrogant, surely? No, it wouldn't. Sobriety is about *reclaiming our specialness*. This has nothing to do with pride or arrogance. It is about loving ourselves and accepting the love being offered to us by other people.

It is not that we think we are better than anyone else; it is also not about thinking we are worse than anyone else. It is about owning who we are and accepting our own worth.

Chloe's story

There is so much to celebrate about getting sober. I can see now that my alcoholism was a sickness of self-destruction. I was terrified of my creative potential. I didn't understand what I was meant to be doing with my life and I didn't want to take responsibility for myself by searching for the answers. When I had ideas, I would deaden them with alcohol because following my dreams might have meant people wouldn't like me.

Thank goodness my body gave up on me, aged thirty. After a string of hospital admissions, I was done. I had to get sober.

I spent the first couple of years of my recovery from alcoholism letting go of destructive relationships and building new friendships with people who only wanted the best things in life for me. Their encouragement rubbed off on me and I started to express my creative desires to them – I told my friends I had always loved creative writing and that I wanted to develop my skills as a writer. I told them I wanted to travel, to help others to recover from addiction, to have a child one day.

I have had the privilege of helping other women to recover from alcoholism – one of the most satisfying creative processes I engage with in my recovery. I will do this for the rest of my life, as it helps me to stay inspired, to feel useful, to stay well myself.

I booked myself on a writing course and it was there that I met my writing mentor – a published author who was overflowing with creativity and generosity of spirit. I started a one-to-one mentoring process with her. I have worked with her for a year and a half now. She is helping me to believe in my abilities as a writer. She is showing me how to find joy in my writing and never to be afraid of expressing myself.

I made the decision to travel round the world, so I worked hard in my career and saved up the money for the trip. As I write this, I am packing up my flat. There are just two weeks until I get on a plane, to start the trip of a lifetime in Asia, Australia and America. I will be able to look my mum in the eyes before I leave and tell her there is nothing to worry about – I care enough about myself these days to keep safe on my travels.

Now, four years into my recovery from alcoholism, I can even look back on the fifteen years when I drank alcoholically and feel total acceptance of that. I have set things right with people I harmed along the way. And I have forgiven myself.

The best thing of all is that I have come to believe that compassion and love are all around me. I have a fascination with nature – it is proof for me of the awe-inspiring creative potential that exists inside every human being. I no longer buy into the scarcity principle – that I need to accept crumbs in life – so in recovery, I feel no difficulty at all in walking away from destructive relationships. I am experiencing true intimacy for the first time in my relationships – I allow people to see my vulnerability and I share my strengths. I believe that I deserve a fulfilling and healthy life, surrounded by people who care about me as if I were a member of their own family.

My mum still worries about me sometimes because she remembers my disappearing for days on end; she remembers the calls from hospitals, the financial chaos, the lies. But with more time, she will see that there is nothing to worry about any more – recovery is way too good to give up.

Chloe, 34, sober since 2007

Living your truth

Chloe is referring to the concept of 'living your truth', or authentic living. Discovering your 'truth' is about living authentically. It's about 'becoming who you really are'. It means that no matter what, you can be true to yourself and what you believe in. It makes life a lot easier in the long run. In sobriety you never have to pretend to be something you're not. You can be who you are, in all your human vulnerabilities and imperfections.

I need to warn you that you won't become perfect when you get sober. I have to tell you that, because I had been under the illusion that one did! I was really disappointed. I thought I would be perfect in every way once I wasn't drinking. But perfection is overrated.

It's through making mistakes and messing up that we learn and grow. The difference in recovery is that we can grow from our mistakes, unlike when we were drinking and we just kept repeating the same ones. As messy as this sounds, it is the juice of life. It is what makes us alive: learning, growing, changing. By doing this, we learn what our 'truth' is. No one can tell you. It is there for you to discover.

Sometimes, the way to discover it is to identify when you have *not* been 'living your truth'. This is sometimes a lot easier to spot. From there you can see what your truth is in any situation. This is not something that happens overnight. Gradually, over time, a path emerged for me and I knew it was the right one because it felt so authentic. I didn't know where it was going, but I trusted, as I took each step forward, that the path would be there.

My story

Sometimes I feel as if I have this power inside me that I can't explain. It feels like an energy, a force that makes me feel energised. It's a feeling of being alive and fully present in my life. It's a feeling of being awake and standing in the sunshine. Living without a drink or a drug is easy. Living life responsibly, from my experience, can sometimes be hard, but it's always worth it.

I am fully responsible for what my life becomes. I may not choose all the events, but I can always choose my response. I met my husband when I was thirty-three. I had a full and happy life and was ready to settle down. I no longer had the limiting belief that I wouldn't be loved, but was patiently waiting for my prince to find me. I met him via the internet, and at the time he lived in America. I wasn't particularly interested in a long-distance relationship, but he assured me he would be moving back to the UK to complete his PhD. We tried to arrange lunch for when he was in London, but with our busy schedules this proved to be difficult. I was about to go on holiday with my friend Heather, so we fixed a date for shortly after my return.

Heather was my best friend; she was also a recovered alcoholic and she knew me like no one else. We were soul sisters and knew each other inside out. We were not two people that you would automatically put together. However, our friendship was very much based on personal and spiritual growth and the journey we took of becoming who we really were. Heather and I went away to Turkey for a break and on the second day she came down with appendicitis. She was rushed into hospital and given emergency surgery. It was not exactly what we had planned but we coped well. It was clear after a few days that she wasn't getting better and eventually I had to fly home and her family flew out. The news was concerning, but I never for an instant considered that she wouldn't get better. Because of all this, I was in two minds about whether to go on this date with Rob as I was so concerned about Heather, but it had been so difficult to arrange I felt that I should go and that Heather would want me to go. Rob and I met on a Monday night in Islington, London, and by the time we'd sat down for dinner, I knew I'd met the man I was going to marry.

The next morning Heather died. I was completely heartbroken and angry that this had happened. It wasn't part of the plan. How could something like this happen to me? I worried that I would never have another friend like her. No one had understood me as well as she did. She knew what I thought before I did. She was completely accepting and non-judgmental of me. She was irreplaceable. But a realisation hit me very quickly. Wherever Heather was, she was fine, and knowing her had taught me the most important lesson in life. What matters most is the people I love and living life to the full.

Having had a friend like Heather enabled me to have future 'soul sisters'. Also, I embraced my relationship with Rob, and opened my heart completely to him. I experienced grief and joy at the same time and that was exactly how it needed to be. As a fully functioning human being I could finally feel the whole spectrum of my emotions, and not want to run away from them. They no longer overwhelmed or frightened me. My grief honoured my love for Heather. It was the natural response to the event, and there was something almost beautiful in its honesty.

Rob was the first man who truly saw my worth. He fell in love with the woman I had become, who had crawled out of the wilderness and into the sunshine.

I know I feel different, really different. I feel the way I always dreamed a human being *should* feel, but never dreamed I would. I feel complete within myself, complete but always changing and growing, and I love the adventure of it. I love pushing myself out of my comfort zones to see what I'm capable of, it's what I live for.

Since I started this way of life, I've never once felt lost or alone or consumed with terror, like I did for so long. In fact, I look back and think how strange that I felt that way for so long, because it's unfathomable to me now. My default programme now is joy.

Of course, I feel frightened, or unsure and confused from time to time. Those are normal human emotions that we have to feel in order to grow. The difference now is that they don't threaten to consume or capsize me the way they did. Even through uncomfortable or challenging feelings I know I'm going to be OK. I know I'll be all right. And that's all I ever wanted: to know that it would all be OK. I often wonder if I had been given a choice and knew beforehand what my life was going to be like, how hard it was going to be, would I have chosen it? Or would I have chosen an easier life, one without the drama, trauma and misery – a life that just 'plodded along'?

Without a doubt I would not change a thing. It is only because of my past that I got the gift of today. Without the challenge of the pain and misery I wouldn't have been forced into seeking something more. And that would have been the greatest tragedy. I could have lived a life without ever being forced into finding out who I really was. I become who I really am on a daily basis. I am becoming. I am growing. I am living.

And the journey is extraordinary. You won't want to miss this for yourself.

I wake up every day with hope and joyous expectation in my belly. I fit in my skin. I feel comfortable in it. I like myself. It doesn't matter what the day is, I look forward to whatever adventure it may contain. I can take the rough with the smooth and embrace it all as a wonderful opportunity to grow.

I don't fear the darkness. There is no emptiness inside me. There is no burning. I am alive. I live to the greatest degree possible.

If you have read this far then picking up this book was no accident, because you too are seeking. The only questions you have to ask yourself are these: are you going to use everything you've learnt, or are you going to go back to sleepwalking? Are you going to wake up and live the life you were meant to have – the life that is waiting for you to claim?

It's your life. Your precious, precious, unique life, unfolding at this very moment. Live it.

References

Alcoholics Anonymous (2001) *The Big Book of Alcoholics Anonymous* World Wide Services Inc.

Alcohol Concern Factsheet (2011) 'Young people and alcohol', Alcohol Concern.

Alcohol Concern Factsheet (2002) 'Alcohol and mental health', Alcohol Concern.

Doweiko H. (2012) *Concepts of Chemical Dependency*, 8th edition, Brook/Cole, Cengage Learning.

Hay, L. (2004) *You Can Heal your Life*, Hay House.

Sharma, R. (2002) *The Saint, the Surfer, the CEO*, Hay House.

Van Deurzen, E. (2002) *Existential Counseling & Psychotherapy*, Sage Publications.

Sources

Jeffers, S, PhD. (1987) *Feel the fear and do it anyway*, Random House.

Moorehead, Melodie K, PhD & Alexander, Cynthia L, PsyD. (2007) 'Transfer of Addiction and Considerations for Preventive Measures in Bariatric Surgery: Part II', Bariatric Times.

Mellody, P, & Miller AW. (2003) *Facing Love Addiction*, HarperCollins.

Millman, D. (1998) *Everyday Enlightenment: Gateways to Human Enlightenment*, Warner Books.

Nay, R. (2004) *Taking Charge of Anger*, The Guilford Press.

Robbins, A. (1992) *Awaken the Giant Within,* Free Press.

Zukav, G, & Francis, L. (2001) *The Heart of the Soul*, Simon & Schuster.

Made in the USA
Las Vegas, NV
20 October 2022

57739262R00106